Public opinion polls and British politics

Public opinion polls and British politics

Richard Hodder-Williams
Department of Politics—University of Bristol

London   Routledge & Kegan Paul

First published 1970
by Routledge & Kegan Paul Ltd
Broadway House, 68–74 Carter Lane
London E.C.4.

Printed in Great Britain by
The Camelot Press Ltd
London and Southampton
and set in Plantin 11 on 12 pt.

ISBN 0 7100 6934 0

Contents

List of tables

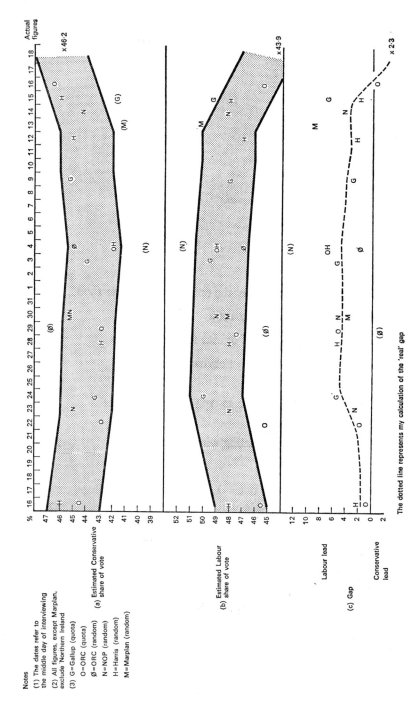

Movement of the polls 16 May–18 June

The dotted line represents my calculation of the 'real' gap

Introduction

It is only in the last ten years or so that public opinion polls have
become an important part of British political life and only in the very
recent past that books on politics have begun to devote whole
chapters to them. This development is exemplified by the Nuffield
studies of general elections in Britain. 'Public Opinion polls,' the
authors of the 1959 study wrote, 'assumed a new prominence in the
1959 election', and in the next study it was stated that 'opinion polls
attained an altogether new level of prominence during the 1959–64
Parliament and . . . had an unquestionable impact on the style in
which the 1964 election was fought'. Apparently 'opinion polls
reached a new level of political importance in the 1964–6 Parliament'.
There seemed no reason to suppose that this progression would not
continue. It was on this assumption that the decision was taken to
write an introductory monograph on opinion polls before another
election flooded the media with ever more statistics from the pollsters.
For there was plenty of room, as the authors of the Nuffield studies
had themselves warned, for clarification on what the polls did, or did
not, indicate.

While it was correctly anticipated that the attention lavished on the
polls would continue to increase, the presumption that Mr Wilson
would wait at least until October 1970 before going to the country
was proved embarrassingly wrong. His decision to hold a general
election in June, ironically due in part to the polls themselves, found
this book already at the printers at a point too late for any major
revisions or additions. Consequently, the main text of this book
remains as it was written in February 1970. But it would have been

absurd to publish a survey of the polls without some specific references to May and June 1970. The main purpose of this Introduction,
therefore, is to consider the apparent 'failure' of the polls at the last
election.

The common belief is that the 1970 general election proved the
pollsters wrong. The final 'predictions' of the polling organizations

Table A   *The final 'predictions' of the opinion polls, June 1970*

	ORC (quota)	Harris (random)	NOP (random)	Gallup (quota)	Marplan (random)	Actual result
Conservative	46·5	46·0	44·1	42·0	41·5	46·2
Labour	45·5	48·0	48·2	49·0	50·2	43·9
Liberal	6·5	5·0	6·4	7·5	7·0	7·7
Others	1·5	1·0	1·3	1·5	1·3	2·2
Conservative lead	+1·0	−2·0	−4·1	−7·0	−8·7	+2·3
Error in lead	1·3	4·3	6·4	9·3	11·9*	—
Average error on major parties	0·95	2·15	3·2	4·6		

(set out in Table A), with the sole exception of Opinion Research
Centre's last and unconventionally weighted figure, implied that the
Labour Party would be returned to power with anything from a com-
fortable to an overwhelming majority. In the event, of course, the
Conservative Party won an overall majority of more than thirty seats.

In an important sense, however, the final poll figures are not necessarily predictions. The figures aggregate the responses to the question,
'At the general election, how do you think you will be likely to vote?'
(the various organizations differ marginally in their wording from this
Harris poll formulation) and show the electorate's *intentions at the
time of interview*. The implication is that these figures predict how the
electorate will vote; but predictions can be accurate only if the voting
intentions conveyed to the interviewers are actually carried out. When
electors behave differently from their stated intentions, the pollsters
may legitimately observe that their final figures were computed from
avowed intentions communicated to them some time before polling

* With the exception of Marplan all these figures exclude Northern Ireland. The only figure excluding Northern Ireland which Marplan was able
to make available to me was the Labour lead, 9·6 per cent.

day and could not therefore take into account respondents' failures to fulfil their earlier intentions. Establishing this basic point is hindered by the pollsters' tendency to congratulate themselves when things go right and to emphasize the accuracy of their predictions in past elections.

Most critical attention has been concentrated on the final predictions—I use this convenient term while acknowledging the caveat in the last paragraph—but we should begin by asking to what extent the pollsters' figures accurately represent the electorate's intentions *at the time of any interview*. The basic difficulty in finding an authoritative answer stems from the lack of any empirical evidence against which to check the published figures for accuracy; after all, polls are conducted precisely because the electorate's intentions are not known. Nevertheless, it is possible to make a reasonable evaluation of the polls if some of the ways in which they can go wrong are considered. There are many ways in which surveys can fail to represent accurately what they attempt to measure—and these are dealt with in later chapters—but three reasons for their apparent failure in 1970 have been most commonly voiced in the letter columns of the national press: that a significant proportion of respondents deceived the interviewers; that the pollsters themselves consciously manipulated their statistics; and, by far the most serious complaint, that their samples were unrepresentative of the electorate at large.

Intentional deception on the part of respondents is of course possible. Clever letters to *The Times* have suggested, with the wisdom of hindsight, that the determined Conservative supporter should have told his interviewer that he was a Labour supporter in order to lull Mr Wilson into a state of false optimism. If this practice was general, all the polls would have suffered from the deception and would have been deceived equally, so they can provide no direct evidence themselves one way or the other on this point. But this is highly unlikely, and not merely because previous surveys have indicated that respondents are essentially truthful (naturally behaviour patterns *can* change). It assumes a level of Machiavellian sophistication among two or three per cent of the electorate, that is the equivalent of 750,000 individual Conservatives throughout the country, which all previous surveys about the interest and commitment of electors suggest is improbable in the extreme.

Nor, in my view, is the second explanation tenable; the polling organizations do not distort their figures for their own political ends. They are in friendly competition with one another and therefore their prime consideration is to be thought more accurate than their rivals. Figure 1 shows how, until the last few days before the election, the findings of the pollsters were broadly similar. Such consistency from separate organizations interviewing separate samples of electors almost certainly reflects the genuineness of their results. Apart from conscientiously polling actual citizens, the only other way by which such consistency could be achieved is a degree of collaboration which the differing political allegiances of the polling executives and their well developed professional pride make unthinkable.

The pollsters, however, did not ignore the possibility that the suspicious would cast doubts on their findings. They had noted that during the 1968 Presidential election in the United States, it seemed as though the status of the newspaper depended very much on its ability to publish a poll. One result of this was that organizations of doubtful expertise and integrity were sometimes commissioned to undertake polls for the less affluent publications and this tended to debase the currency of the serious polls' findings. Either all the findings were accepted with a complacent lack of discrimination as the authentic representation of the American people's intentions, or they were dismissed with equally undiscriminating contempt as wholly unreliable. The lack of seriousness with which the polls might be taken persuaded Research Services not to undertake their usual series of predictive polls before the general election and on 21 May the executives of the remaining major polling organizations met to draft a *Code of Practice for Opinion Polls*.

Apart from noting the statistical limitations of sample surveys and the range within which precision might be expected, the statement issued at the end of the meeting laid down that every substantial published report of poll findings should give the sampling method used, the size of the sample, and the dates of the fieldwork. In addition, further information, for example about the proportion of those originally selected for a sample who were actually contacted or the wording of the questionnaire itself, should be made available on request to interested journalists, academics, and political leaders. Discussion with the operatives, cursory glances at the piles of completed questionnaires encountered in the organizations' corridors, and the testimony of those actually involved in the fieldwork make it clear that the polls' executives take their jobs seriously and do not 'doctor' the results. This is not to say that everything is perfect. Some interviewers may falsify a few of their questionnaires; the results of the surveys are not always presented by the news media in an unbiased way; and the organizations themselves do sometimes search for the statistics which will gladden the hearts of the professionals at Central

Office or in Transport House. To take one example, the ORC hand-outs appeared to be looking for a Conservative victory and their copy was slanted accordingly. The basic survey was always scrupulously reported, but the figures were then reworked on the very sound premiss that not all those who expressed a party preference would in fact vote. By discovering which of their sample were determined to vote or felt the result of the election to be of great importance to them, ORC were able to reduce the crude lead given to the Labour Party in the original survey. While this was, on the whole, a new development, it was not unique to ORC nor did it involve any reworking that was of dubious validity or hidden from the *Evening Standard*'s readers.

The third reason put forward for the failure of the polls, and the one which must be taken most seriously, was that the samples were unrepresentative of the electorate. There is a discussion of the basic principles of sampling elsewhere in this book. All that requires saying at this stage is that, for the purposes of discovering the electorate's party allegiance, a sample of 2,000 will, as long as there is no bias caused by respondents' conscious deception, provide an accurate estimate of the major parties' strength to within 2 per cent—plus or minus—in 95 cases out of 100. In other words, when a poll indicates that 46 per cent of the electorate intend to vote Labour, one can be 95-per-cent certain that the actual percentage figure lies somewhere between 44 and 48. This means that we should *expect* not only that one survey in twenty will be hopelessly out but that there will be minor variations within the remaining nineteen surveys. Curiously enough a poll is just as suspect when it is consistently 'right' as when it is frequently 'wrong'. Those who have convinced themselves that samples of 2,000 are inadequate for estimating the intentions of the whole electorate are unlikely to be persuaded by assertions based upon probability theory; nor will those who believe that the polls' findings are invalidated by their own failure to know any actual respondents be comforted by the observation that if the polling organizations continued to poll as frequently as they do it would take about 500 years for everyone to be interviewed even once! The theoretical arguments justifying confidence in the ability of sample surveys to produce accurate estimations of whole populations must be accepted; at the same time, however, it should be remembered that their statistics are only estimations and perfect accuracy should never be expected.

Figure 1 plots the polls' findings from 16 May to 18 June 1970. Starting from the assumption that the polls were likely to be accurate within the plus or minus 2-per-cent range, I have shaded in a band 4-per-cent wide which includes as many findings as possible. Since five organizations were concurrently carrying out independent surveys (some based upon random samples, others upon quota samples), the high degree of agreement shown should give us confidence that, unless there was some common bias affecting all the polls, the 'real' proportion of the electorate intending to vote for either of the two major parties will be found within the shaded bands.

But what about the findings outside the bands ? There seem to be four samples which fall into this category, of which the most dramatic was NOP's figure of a 12·4 per cent Labour lead barely a fortnight before the election. Although NOP's sample seemed perfectly representative at first glance, in that it contained the correct proportion of people from each occupational class, sex group, and so on, a closer inspection after publication showed that *within* each class there were important imbalances. For example, the skilled manual class in the sample seemed to be less likely to be house owners, telephone subscribers, or car owners than might have been expected from national statistics. It may also have been that clustering, the system of limiting the random selection of respondents to the confines of part of one ward rather than to the whole constituency, exaggerated the tendency by failing to sample enough different kinds of skilled manual workers' homes. It is this sort of imbalance which inevitably affects a sample every so often. Marplan's final survey also appears to have been the product of a skewed sample, but it is difficult to discover exactly where the bias lay. Marplan ask fewer personal questions than NOP, so that it is impossible to check whether the sample was skewed *within* the occupational classes in the way NOP's had been. And the same is probably true of ORC's random sample in the *Sunday Times* of 1 June which showed, quite against the trend of all the other polls, a lead for the Conservatives. Gallup, which seems to have suffered worst from the comeback against the pollsters, felt that their last sample may also have been skewed; but here too it proved difficult to pinpoint the cause of the bias. Unfortunately for the pollsters, two of the skewed samples were final samples and this is exactly what they fear most. While bias undoubtedly crept into some of the samples in one way or another, this is insufficient to account for the extent of their predictive errors, for even those samples which appear to be free from bias still favoured the Labour Party to the extent of forecasting the wrong winner—and that is a crime for which no pollster is easily forgiven.

A simple method of accounting for the major part of the polls' errors is the hypothesis that a rapid decline in the fortunes of the Labour Party took place in the last days of the campaign and consequently a sudden narrowing of the gap until the Conservatives nosed ahead in the last day or two. This is represented graphically in Figure 1. It will be noticed that the proportion of the electorate claiming to be Conservative supporters throughout the campaign was very much in line with the final figures. The decline in support for the Labour Party was far more marked. Two explanations for this can be considered. First, many Labour incliners indicated their preference to the interviewers but did not act when the election day came; this problem of Labour abstainers and differential turnout lies behind the tendency to exaggerate Labour support which was observable, although to a lesser degree, in 1966 as well. Second, many Labour incliners actually changed their party preference in the last few days, some moving into the Conservative camp and some lending their support to one of the minor parties.

By testing these possibilities ORC was able to predict a Conservative victory. What happened was this. The main part of the interviewing for ORC's final and dramatic poll was carried out between the Saturday and Monday before polling day. Following the release of disappointing trade figures and the Conservatives' concerted attack on the Labour Government's economic record, ORC reinterviewed 300 of their original sample, the last reinterviews not being completed until Wednesday. They found that there was a marked weakening in Labour support, which was corroborated by the private polls they were undertaking for the Conservative Party. The original survey had shown a 4·5 per cent lead for Labour (marginally higher than the figures NOP and Harris were coming up with), but this was corrected on the assumption that the trend shown by the reinterviews, and other findings as well, was common to the whole sample. The new calculation indicated a dead-heat. The final prediction of a Conservative victory was based on the polls' findings that Conservative supporters were significantly more determined to vote than Labour supporters. In this way ORC predicted the winning party correctly, though even so they underestimated the margin of the Conservatives' success.

NOP, as they had done in 1966, also weighted their final figures to take account of reinterviews. A random sample of 1,562 drawn from those interviewed in the first two surveys of the campaign were reinterviewed between Friday and Tuesday and the extent of the net change discovered was applied to the whole of the first two samples. Most of this reinterviewing, however, took place before the Monday trade figures and devaluation scares had hit the headlines and so the late swing away from Labour was not sufficiently noticed. NOP, like most of the other polling organizations, recognized that differential turnout might be significant; on 7 June it was suggested that the 5·5 per cent Labour lead might be cut to 2 per cent if that was taken into consideration, and their final prediction was accompanied by the comment that, allowing for the effects of the postal vote and differential turnout, Labour's lead might be a bare 2 per cent. This, I think, would have been a very close estimation of intentions at the time the last round of interviews was undertaken.

The Harris poll too was slightly unorthodox. The final sample was weighted in favour of the thirty-two marginal constituencies out of the 120 used for the national survey. Although the extra interviews carried out in these special constituencies indicated a tiny majority for the Conservatives, the overall figure came out as a 2 per cent Labour lead. Attention was drawn to the Conservatives' better organization, but no recalculations were made. After all, accurate predictions had been achieved without recourse to such techniques before, and it would have been slightly curious if the established polling organizations had changed their methods, especially since they had proved so successful in the past. But it is probably true to say that in previous elections the pollsters had been fortunate in that people do not seem to have changed their minds late in the campaign. The new approach in times of greater volatility is an improvement. By asking respondents how determined they are to vote and how deeply they care about the result of the election, the pollsters will be able to calculate quite accurately who will actually vote and who will probably abstain. Obviously, too, the later the interviewing is undertaken, the more likely an accurate indication of the electorate's behaviour will emerge.

While this is not the place to try to answer in detail why people changed their party allegiance in the last few days or to discover the exact extent of Labour abstentions, some consideration of these factors is necessary to any estimation of the polls' performances. The lowest turnout in an election since 1945 suggests that, holiday-making notwithstanding, there was a substantial degree of non-voting; since Labour incliners were found on the whole to be less determined to vote than Conservative supporters, it seems reasonable to suppose that an error of 2 per cent in the gap between the parties can be accounted for by abstentions, which varied clearly from area to area. There certainly appeared to be a slackening off in Labour's activities in the last few days of the campaign which may well have had an effect on the party's success in getting their vote out. It would be appropriate in this election to find a parallel from the World Cup which vied for, and often dominated, news coverage in the mass media. And indeed there are striking similarities in the way England lost against West Germany and Labour was overhauled by the Conservatives. In both instances, the initiative was surrendered and the late runners, by being allowed to attack consistently, ultimately exploited the weaknesses in their opponents' defences. Having lost the initiative, neither England nor the Labour Party found the momentum or the luck in the time available to regain the advantage they had squandered.

Such an interpretation may be too clever and neat. But there are indications that there was this movement of opinion. Marplan surveys in the Midlands, although they were less accurate than some of their constituency surveys have been in the past, found that the swing to the Conservatives had trebled in a week; ORC, and Conservative Central Office researches, indicated a late swing from Labour; so did NOP's reinterviews, particularly those conducted after the Monday; and Gallup's early post-election fieldwork confirmed this pattern. There seems little doubt that considerations of the economy played a major part in this realignment of allegiance. It had been the belief, assiduously fostered by Labour leaders, that the economy and the balance of payments had improved which accounted for the swing back to the Labour Party in the early spring; and now, with some seemingly unfavourable trade figures and talk of a wage freeze and a further devaluation, some of the electorate forsook their recent and far from deep-seated support for Labour, recollected the days of apparent austerity and economic crisis which had been the public hallmark of the Labour Government, and returned to the Conservative ranks. Throughout the election it was the cost of living which the electorate deemed the most important issue and the Conservatives were ultimately thought to be better at keeping it down. Furthermore, the polls indicated not only that a majority of electors believed the dire warnings of Mr Heath that another economic crisis was at hand, but they believed the Conservatives were the best party to deal with it; significantly, before the Monday trade figures it had been the Labour Party which had been thought more competent at setting the economy in order.

Implicit in this analysis, of course, is the belief that the polls provide essentially reliable information about what the electorate is thinking. It is not only confidence in probability theory and the past record of the pollsters which support this position. On the day of the election itself a market research firm called Taylor, Nelson and Associates conducted a survey for the BBC at Gravesend, which had been designated by the Nuffield College computers as the most 'average' constituency in Great Britain. They interviewed a sample of electors *after* they had voted, thus eliminating the difficulties of differential turnout and late changes in party preference, and their figures almost exactly matched the actual constituency result. In favourable circumstances, therefore, polls can be very accurate. Although the polling organizations' records can be defended and their errors largely explained away, their divergence in the last few days before the election cannot be shrugged off without some feelings of uneasiness. It would be reassuring if one could be *certain* that the final Marplan and Gallup predictions were definitely based upon the sort of sampling bias which must be expected from time to time.

It has not been the polls alone which have taken something of a knock. Two conventional wisdoms have been tarnished. First, it was generally held that a Prime Minister had a distinct, and some would say unfair, advantage over the Opposition in his ability to call an election at whatever moment the opinion polls indicated to be the most favourable. This thesis was refurbished and re-emphasized in 1970 by pessimistic Conservatives who felt that they were going to be cheated of a victory they believed to be rightfully theirs. In the event, of course, the barometer of public feeling on which Mr Wilson based his judgment to go to the country—and I am sure it *was* the poll findings which crystallized his decision to go for a summer election— failed to anticipate the late swing away from Labour. So the salutary lesson was taught that elections are concerned ultimately with people, fickle and unpredictable though they may be, and not with the seemingly inexorable statistics of opinion polls.

Second, the general feeling that the Presidential nature of British elections had given a decisive advantage to the party whose champion is most popular among the electorate must now be reconsidered. Although Mr Wilson normally refused to comment on poll findings, he allowed himself once to observe to a reporter during the campaign: 'Perhaps you can point to the last occasion on which a party won with its leader trailing behind the other leader in personal ratings— particularly if you find he was trailing nearly two to one behind the other leader. It is a good law.' Such an evaluation is no longer acceptable.

Both these developments, it seems to me, are healthy. The mass media's obsessive concern with the polls in the 1970 election tended to divert attention from the basic purpose of the election campaign which is not to guess the victorious party but to project the ideals, policies, and leaders of the parties from which the electorate is to choose the next government. Symptomatic of this concern was the unprecedented way in which the newspapers reported each other's polls. More important, however, was the way in which the headlines often reflected not the essential issues on which the election might have been fought but the 'state of the race', encouraging the paper's party to make a final effort to pass its rival in the home straight. This metaphorical language reflects the style of much of the reporting. The pollsters should not be blamed for this unuseful approach; their activities were geared to their sponsors' demands for something specific, a regular series of predictions. And there is some evidence to support the view that the publication of polls did boost sales, for people came to know, for example, when the next Gallup poll was due for publication and bought a paper accordingly.

Whether this continuous emphasis on the polls' predictions affected voting behaviour itself is another matter. The original band-wagon thesis can now be laid quietly to rest. Not only did the published polls indicate a clear and large Labour victory, the people themselves believed that Labour would win, so that by the last ORC poll, for example, 77 per cent of the sample expected a Labour victory. And yet the Conservatives won comfortably. It may be, however, that more subtle pressures were at work. It is tempting, but dangerous, to generalize from personal observations, but it would not surprise me to discover that the certainty of the polls not only gave Labour voters and party workers an overconfidence bordering on complacency—and there is some evidence that the party machine did tend to free-wheel towards the end of the campaign—but also persuaded some people to express their freedom of choice by voting against the polls. Unfortunately, it is highly unlikely that any relevant and reliable data to substantiate or refute such a hunch will be forthcoming. The general failure of the polls to name the eventual winner correctly may make newspaper editors less eager to publicize every prediction in the future; but I suspect that this will not be the case.

To concentrate almost exclusively on the predictive function of the polls as I have done in this Introduction is an unfortunate necessity. Far more important is the light opinion polls may be able to throw upon the views, prejudices and aspirations of the common man. Already the representative nature of the polls' findings have percolated through to the highest levels of decision making. Debates in both Houses of Parliament now frequently make mention of the findings of opinion polls and serious television programmes like *Panorama* commission polling organizations to carry out surveys on topics like the repatriation of immigrants which are to be discussed on television. Even editors have to substantiate with statistics their interpretations of what the public is thinking. While it is right that these developments have taken place and that the people who do not form the decision-making élite have a chance for their views to be heard, the interpretation of the polls' findings on the Common Market, for example, or the appropriate weight to be given to public opinion in reaching governmental decisions, is open to debate. The purpose of this monograph is to set out the sort of considerations which should be taken into account before acting upon the findings of the pollsters.

Two things should be made clear at the outset. First, this is an introductory book. It is concerned with the measurement of public opinion and the extent to which statistics genuinely reflect the attitudes and beliefs of the general public; some reference must therefore be made to the statistical techniques employed by the polling organizations. But no attempt is made to provide a detailed overview of the sophisticated methods developed by social scientists to study political behaviour. Their findings, however, are used to illustrate some of the strengths and weaknesses of their more ordinary cousins, the polls published regularly in some of the national newspapers.

Second, the emphasis on this book is on the practical. It is not concerned, therefore, with the formation of public opinion (important though that is as a field of study), but with the interpretation and the impact of the statistics purporting to measure it. Interpretation, of course, cannot be wholly divorced from the way in which opinions are formed and expressed. But my main interest is to discover how accurately the opinion polls represent general opinion, how far governments ought to act in accordance with the opinions thus represented, and in what ways the publication of those opinions has actually affected the working of the British political system.

There is a final point. A book of this kind must inevitably be topical and some of it is bound to be slightly out of date within a short space of time. The practice of politics is always changing. The facts and figures presented in the main text are, as far as I can tell, correct as at 1 January 1970. For helping me correct any errors in the original draft I am indebted to several people, particularly my colleagues at Bristol University and the executives of the polling organizations who talked and corresponded with me. The errors that remain, it is both proper and true to say, are of course my own responsibility.

Nairobi, 11 August 1970

1

Preliminaries

Public Opinion Polls claim to measure public opinion. This is, however, a deceptively simple statement which requires some clarification. To begin with, the term Public Opinion Poll is often used to describe the findings of surveys not strictly concerned with opinions at all. The Gallup questionnaire reproduced as the Appendix contains questions seeking factual information both about the past and the present, as well as others concerned with intended behaviour at some hypothetical general election in the future, or personal opinions on matters open to controversy. In the second place, public opinion itself appears to mean different things to different people, so that it is important to be quite clear how the pollsters define what they claim to measure.

Varieties of polls

It is possible to trace the antecedents of the Public Opinion Polls which appear regularly in some of the daily newspapers at least as far back as the end of the last century, to Charles Booth's classical seventeen-volume study of poverty in London. 'My object,' Booth wrote, 'has been to show the numerical relation which poverty, misery and depravity bear to regular earnings and comparative comfort' (Booth, 1889–1902, i.5). The pollsters of today are equally determined to establish numerical relationships, to assess what proportion of their respondents clean their teeth, vote for the Labour Party, believe that capital punishment should be reintroduced, or whatever the particular survey is concerned about. Although statistical techniques have advanced enormously since Booth's day —it was not until 1912, with Bowley's study of working-class conditions in Reading, that the methodological advance of sampling was first used (Bowley, 1913)—the approach used both by Booth and the present pollsters with their highly sophisticated processes is essentially a quantitative one. Information so gained, it was thought, would provide a far more reliable guide to actual conditions than people's impressions. The fundamental point about polls is that they are not impressionistic but quantitative, and aspire to a degree of scientific accuracy.

Some writers have drawn a distinction between polls and surveys. Polls, they maintain, 'divide people with engaging simplicity into the "yes", "no" and "don't know" categories', while surveys delve much deeper, for example into the intensity with which opinions are held (Abrams and Rose, 1960, 7). While it is important to differentiate between questions which allow the respondent a number of choices and questions which do not, common usage has made this particular terminology less helpful than it may once have been. If we clung to that distinction, our Gallup questionnaire would be both poll and survey, a confusion which it is better to avoid. The most famous poll of all, the Gallup Poll, is in fact run by a company called Social Surveys (Gallup Poll) Ltd, which epitomizes the intimate link between surveys and polls. Since both types of question are asked in a single interview and the results published at the same time, it is most convenient merely to be aware that questions can be framed in a number of ways but not to employ two different terms. Thus I shall use the terms survey and poll as virtual synonyms, to indicate a systematic process of collating and collecting responses, of whatever complexity, from a sample of the public.

However, I think it is useful to distinguish between three general subject areas in which surveys ask questions. While these can be separated analytically, most surveys involve questions of all three types, as in fact our Gallup survey does. First, there are those questions which attempt to gather specific, factual information. In some cases, notably in the field of market research, the respondent has direct access to the information. To the question, 'What toothpaste do you use?' ignorance can be circumvented by a rapid visit to the bathroom. The accuracy to be expected from respondents on questions of this type is relatively high, since the answers can usually be empirically discovered if they are not already known. There are, however, occasions when a respondent may have access to the specific information but be unwilling to divulge it; surveys of family expenditure, for example, may well run into this trouble. In other cases, as with questions enquiring about the past, verification is not so simple, since it is not always possible to have direct access to the answer. 'For which party did you vote at the last election?' seems a straight-forward factual question about the past, but it is not always easily answered. One respondent in a survey I conducted in Rhodesia, when asked how she had voted in the 1962 territorial election, replied vehemently that she had never voted for the Rhodesian Front and never would vote for them, but that in 1962 she had voted for Mr Winston Field. It so happened that Mr Field, himself a well-known local man, had been *leader* of the Rhodesian Front at the time! The same failure of recollection has been observed in Britain (Allen, 1966). More detailed questions, for example about the number of years of formal education a respondent may have had, are still less easy to be accurate about. Another respondent in my survey main-tained that he had had sixteen years of formal education between the years of seven and nineteen! Questions of fact do have their problems, then, problems of recall, of honesty perhaps or comprehension, but, except in the most unfavourable conditions, the respondent can give his answers from knowledge and in many cases he can actually verify his response. But this is not the case with the subject matter of other types of question.

The second category of question attempts to gather information about intentions, in particular about the way people are going to vote at some future election. Polls based on this kind of question, then, aim to predict how the electorate will cast its votes. Since they are dealing with what is yet to happen, it is impossible for many people to know how they are going to vote. All the pollster can do is to assume that he received truthful answers and state what the electorate's present intention with respect to future action is. Only the last poll before an election can be checked against objective data for validity. These predictive polls form the subject of Chapter 3.

Finally, there are those questions which attempt to gather informa-tion about opinions, as distinct from facts or intentions. Opinions cannot be empirically verified as facts can be; nor can they be checked against empirical evidence in the same way as intentions. Furthermore, opinions are more variegated and complicated than pieces of specific factual information and can be the expression of a much greater variety of positions than the act of voting, where the choice open to an elector is limited and known. Thus respondents may be unclear about the exact opinion they hold on a given issue and pollsters may feel unable to accept responses at their face value yet be denied objective criteria against which to verify the opinions they disbelieve. These polls, in a sense the true opinion polls, are considered in Chapter 4.

Polls, as I have already pointed out, aspire to a degree of scientific accuracy. This does not mean that they expect to achieve the accuracy and certainty of which the natural sciences are frequently capable, but it does emphasize that no discussion of polls can be divorced from judgments on their accuracy. So far, we have noted two difficulties; the inability of the respondent to know the answer and his possible unwillingness to communicate a true answer. The range and variety of the polls' subject-matter affects the extent to which these difficulties prevent an accurate representation of the particular objects being measured. This problem is in fact a central theme of the next two chapters.

It is not unreasonable at this stage to draw up a tentative scheme to indicate the accuracy interviewers might expect from responses to questions in these three categories. The highest level of accuracy would be reserved for factual questions the answers to which can be easily checked empirically; the level of accuracy is likely to diminish as verification becomes less easy for the respondent and the facts sought less accessible. Lower still would come answers to predictive polls, since there is probably a greater element of uncertainty in such cases; answers to these questions cannot be known by the respondent in the same way as events in the past which have been directly experienced. On the other hand, behaviour may be so much part of habit that future actions can be predicted with a very high degree of certainty in individual cases, and this perhaps applies to voting intentions for many people. A lower level of accuracy still would be expected from questions about opinions, where there is no possibility of verification, since opinions are exclusive to the holder alone. The least accurate replies of all would probably result from questions on topics personally embarrassing to the respondent, although even in these cases questionnaire technique has so advanced that many of the respondents' inhibitions can be overcome. Obviously there will be blurring at the margin; a convinced nuclear disarmer will 'know' his opinion about Polaris submarines more accurately than an old lady will know in what year she moved into the district. But there is, as a general rule, a progression in the level of accuracy to be expected, with embarrassing personal questions at the bottom and simple factual questions at the top. The polls with which we are concerned fill the middle ground and include subjects where a very high and a very low level of accuracy may be expected.

The problem of defining public opinion

There is little to be gained by entering the controversy of what properly constitutes an opinion. According to Albig's seminal work on public opinion, an opinion 'is some expression on a controversial point' (Albig, 1939, 1). This cannot be accepted as a universal definition, but it does draw attention to two of the most important characteristics of the pollsters' subject-matter. First of all, an opinion for the pollster can only be something which is expressed. It is this need for an opinion to be communicated that makes Albig's definition (and other political scientists in this field have reiterated it) unacceptable as a general rule; for it is surely the case that men hold opinions in the common sense of the word without actually expressing them. It is probably better to say that an opinion should be communicable rather than actually communicated. But not everything that can be communicated is an opinion. A distinction needs to be made, for example, between a man who claims that Guyana is in Africa, a statement demonstrably incorrect (although possibly of great interest to the pollster), and a man who declares that the death penalty should be reintroduced, a pronouncement which can provoke genuine disagreements but which is not susceptible to tests about its truth or falsity. For our present purposes, then, an opinion may be satisfactorily defined as an expression, either actual or potential, on a topic admitting of controversy.

But this still leaves unresolved the definition of *public* opinion. Most writers seem to imply one or more of the following definitions. First, public opinion consists of the views expressed on a given topic by a public; second, public opinion, by an analogy with public interest or public parks, is the opinion common to the public; and third, public opinion consists of whatever views a community makes public. Let us deal with each of these in turn.

To many sociologists, a public is an amorphous social structure, whose members share a community of interest but probably not formal or personal connections with each other. Thus one can speak of the motoring public or the gardening public; in fact, a single individual may be a member of as many publics as he has interests. Public opinion can then be defined as the opinions held by any public. If this approach is to be employed usefully, obviously the exact reference group must be clearly stated. For pollsters in Britain, the reference group is usually the political community whose common interest lies in being enfranchised citizens of Great Britain (most surveys seem to exclude Northern Ireland), but in special cases the public whose opinion is canvassed is somewhat more limited, geographically as at by-elections or occupationally as with Trade Unionists. As a rule, pollsters make it quite clear what public's opinion they are attempting to discover; for the most part their public, which I shall now refer to as *the* public, is the nation's electorate.

The second definition centres on the idea that opinions are held by the public in common. (It was not until the twentieth century that the public became equated with the mass of citizenry.) The public interest, public corporations, public conveniences and their like imply that they are common to all, and so, by analogy, public opinion becomes some kind of reified General Will. This rather extreme view is not satisfactory, partly because the individual members of the public as a matter of fact do not always hold similar views, and partly because, by implying that opinions become instantaneously universalized, it is incompatible with what we know about the communication of ideas. Usually, however, the definition is made more acceptable by a simple modification. Thus Lowell can write that, for public opinion to be said to exist, 'a majority is not enough, and unanimity is not required, but the opinion must be such that while the minority may not share it, they feel bound, by conviction, not by fear, to accept it' (Lowell, 1919, 15–16). The majoritarian overtone of this definition finds particular favour with practising politicians and newspaper editors because its democratic implications lend support to their own attempts to influence government action. This concept, by implying that public opinion can be used meaningfully in the singular, like that of the nation's will, is essentially metaphorical.

The third definition distinguishes between public and private opinion, so that public opinion is defined as the opinions which people are prepared to make public. Public opinion in this sense is an overt act and is not necessarily a candid reflection of a man's private opinion (Harrisson, 1940). It can be seen that this is virtually the equivalent of Albig's definition of an opinion pure and simple, but there is something unsatisfactory in failing to distinguish clearly between a view which is potentially communicable (but known only to the holder) and a view which is actually communicated (and thus known to others). A man's public utterances may well fail to reflect his innermost thoughts. It is useful to develop this analysis further by differentiating between the expressions of opinion made on a man's own initiative and those elicited only after questioning by friends or interviewers. This distinction is in fact a fundamental one, since it helps to explain the disparate concepts of public opinion employed by pollsters and some academic writers.

The pollsters are moderately clear about their own definition of public opinion. 'Public opinion,' Henry Durant has written, 'can be considered to mean what the pollers say it means . . . a conventional yardstick which imparts to one person an opinion more or less equal in weight to the opinion of other individual persons' (Durant, 1955, 151). This definition accepts the mid-twentieth century democratic imperative of one man, one vote, one value and transcribes it into a new formula: one man, one opinion, one value. The public, as I have already pointed out, thus becomes in most cases co-extensive with the electorate; this public does not necessarily have one opinion as though some form of General Will existed, but a number of opinions, one of which may or may not be held by a majority; finally, these opinions are made public to interviewers on request and are not volunteered. On the other hand, Lord Windlesham, in his study of reactions to Britain's attempted entry into the Common Market, wrote quite firmly that 'public opinion is not a democratic affair of one man, one vote' (Windlesham, 1966, 154). And the American V. O. Key has defined public opinion as 'those opinions held by private persons which Governments find it prudent to heed' (Key, 1961, 14). For Windlesham, Durant's public is too extensive; for Key, it is too undifferentiated.

The basic reason for this is that Windlesham and Key are both thinking of public opinion as a dynamic concept, as a force in politics which actually affects the Government's decisions. In fact, Windlesham calls attention to just this when he distinguishes between the positive public opinion of the few and the negative public opinion of the many (Windlesham, 1966, 155). Newspaper editors are also happier in this idiom, since they too are concerned with the influence that can be exerted on a Government. There remains, nevertheless, the perhaps uncharitable suspicion that editors' public opinion is in reality private opinion masquerading as public. After the Roskill Commission reported against Stansted as the best site for London's third airport, the newspapers were full of references to the triumph of 'public opinion', but the public whose opinions had been influential was nowhere nearly as extensive as the pollsters'. Thinking of public opinion as a dynamic concept was the common practice until the advent of the pollsters and was clearly connected with theories of government which did not accept the egalitarian principles of the later twentieth century (Speier, 1950: Childs 1965). It can be easily recognized as one of the forces which drove Sir Samuel Hoare from office in 1936 and which buoyed up the leader-writers in their support of Neville Chamberlain in 1938. This positive public opinion is usually volunteered and, above all, incalculable, since it is not quite clear who exactly constitutes the informed 'public'. It is in fact a synthesis of one public's views, the opinion-leaders', dependent for its influence more on the status of its holders than on their quantity.

There is no single correct definition of public opinion. It is necessary, however, to be aware that the expression can be, and is, used in a variety of ways. One's preference depends very much on the questions one wishes to ask. To those social scientists interested in the processes of decision-making, the dynamic concept may seem appropriate; to those interested in the extent to which governments are responsive to their constituents' wishes, the pollsters' concept may seem appropriate. The public opinion which I have chosen to investigate is this latter concept. Since, unlike the dynamic concept, it is essentially calculable, the procedures by which it is calculated must be the first subject for comment.

2

Pollsters and polling

One indication of the growing importance attached to public opinion polls since 1945 is the increase in the number of organizations conducting polls. Whereas in 1945 only Gallup predicted the general election result, six organizations were concerned with the 1970 election. It is probably appropriate to sketch their various histories and procedures at the outset of this discussion. Their figures, which purport to tell us what the nation is thinking or intending, are not derived from interviews with every citizen, but with a sample of the citizenry. Thus our second task is to consider the methods by which they choose their samples, since they are of great importance in deciding the extent to which we should accept the findings as a true representation of the opinions of all the citizens. Apart from the problems raised by random or quota sampling, there are other general difficulties with which pollsters are faced and with which we should be familiar. And finally, since statistics are not self-evident truths, some thought must be given to the ways in which they are presented and then interpreted.

The polling organizations

The organizations which carry out surveys of public opinion spend barely five per cent of their resources on such surveys. The vast bulk of their activity is concerned with what is often referred to indiscriminately as market research. This umbrella phrase conceals a number of quite distinct fields in which work is carried out; most companies in fact distinguish between at least four areas of activity.

First, and probably most important, is the market research carried out for commercial companies into the public's attitude towards certain of their products. Second, special studies of social problems are increasingly being carried out, for government departments, for local authorities and for bodies like the Institute of Race Relations or research teams at universities. These often require special techniques and usually involve a public much smaller than the whole nation. Third, there are surveys undertaken to discover the general public's attitude towards particular national topics. Finally, there is a small amount of straight predictive polling. It is with the last two categories, which I shall call political polling, that we are concerned; but it must be remembered that this polling is but a tiny part of the work of the polling organizations, and several of them in fact usually include predictive questions, political questions, social questions and commercial questions in the same survey.

The Gallup Poll is the oldest of the British polling organizations. In 1936, after Dr George Gallup had predicted Roosevelt's victory in the American Presidential election, Dr Henry Durant set up the British Institute of Public Opinion following Dr Gallup's procedures. Its first findings, published in the *News Chronicle*, appeared in 1937. Although there are close connections with the parent organization in America, the BIPO, or Social Surveys (Gallup Poll) Ltd as it is now known, has complete financial and managerial independence. In 1963, it became a wholly-owned subsidiary of S. G. Warburg, the merchant bankers, but in 1969 Warburg sold out to Swedish and French Gallup. The organization functioned throughout the war, but only achieved credibility in 1945 when it surprised so many commentators, including its publishers, by forecasting a Labour victory in the general election. With the demise of the *News Chronicle* in 1960, its findings have since been published in the *Daily Telegraph*. In contrast to its earliest days, over 95 per cent of its work is outside the area of political polling. It produces a private subscription bulletin which contains the details of most of the company's political research, and retains the data gleaned from these surveys which can be consulted on request; a considerable amount of academic work on voting behaviour owes its statistical backing to the company's files. In addition, it has undertaken separate survey work for Government departments, both major political parties, and some academics.

The Gallup Poll's most obvious claim to fame, however, lies in its adherence to the method of quota sampling. It is still the major polling organization, now that the *Daily Express* Poll no longer exists, to use this method for its regular political polling. A survey is undertaken each week; but only one of them—normally the one carried out in the middle of the month—is actually published in the *Daily Telegraph*. However, it does not use quota samples exclusively. It carries out regular random sample surveys, but the findings from these are only published in the weeks immediately preceding a general election. In the four weeks before the 1966 election, for example, both polls were published; the quota sample proved to be the more accurate. In 1970 the results of the random sample were not published.

National Opinion Polls, the second organization to publish a monthly predictive poll, was founded in 1958 as a subsidiary company of Associated Newspapers. Although it still does media research for the holding company, its independent research activities occupy at least ninety per cent of its time and in 1968 it changed its name to NOP Market Research Ltd. It usually carries out a political survey fortnightly, although sometimes less frequently, but only one is used for the monthly publication in the *Daily Mail*. Like Gallup, NOP produces a private subscription bulletin which gives the results of its political surveys in rather greater detail than that offered by the newspaper. It entered the electoral lists in 1959 and undertook regular political polling with its own field organization in 1961 using the method of quota sampling. In October 1963, it changed to random sampling. It carried out some research for the Conservative Party before the 1964 election and one of its directors, Humphrey Taylor, was encouraged by the party to set up his own research organization, now called Opinion Research Centre. NOP continues to do work for political parties, Government Departments, Local Authorities, Universities and Regional Planning Boards. Its survey material provided the statistical backing for the North Regional Planning Committee's study of leisure activities in the North Region as well as subsidiary material for David Butler and Donald Stoke's *Political Change in Britain*.

Research Services Ltd grew out of the research department of the advertising agency London Press Exchange. It became a separate and autonomous company in 1946 while remaining a subsidiary of the holding company, the London Press Exchange Group, from which it derives only five per cent of its work. In July 1969, the major parts of the Group were bought by an American Company, but Research Services Ltd remains a subsidiary of the small holding company, Lopex Ltd. As with the other organizations, political polling forms only a very small part of the company's work. Its political career originated with a not very successful prediction of the 1951 election (published in the *Daily Graphic*), but more recent predictions have been very accurate indeed. While predictive polling and simple opinion polling are undertaken, almost all the company's work is concerned with market research and special studies of social problems. Its research lay behind the pinpointing of 'target voters' in the early 1960s, and it was responsible for the research work on such studies as *Must Labour Lose*? (Abrams and Rose), *Angels in Marble* (McKenzie and Silver), *Relative Deprivation and Social Justice* (Runciman), *The Civic Culture* (Almond and Verba), and PEP's study of racial discrimination in Britain. A considerable amount of its activities have been for government departments and the company carries out the annual national readership survey. At present, the company is not associated with any newspaper, although surveys were regularly carried out for the *Observer* in 1967 and 1968. Surveys are normally based upon the principle of random sampling, although on occasions, particularly for market research, quota samples are also used. The company decided not to conduct surveys for the 1970 elections.

Marplan Ltd grew out of the research department of McCann, Erickson Advertising, itself a subsidiary of Interpublic Ltd. It became a separate company in 1959 and autonomous, although still a subsidiary of Interpublic Ltd, in 1962. The vast majority of its work is conventional market research, but it has now joined the ranks of the major political polling organizations. In 1968, the company agreed to carry out quarterly surveys for *The Times*. It first carried out a study into electoral attitudes in 1962 (this was published by the *Sunday Times* in 1963) and it did some constituency predictions in the 1966 general election for the *Sunday Times* and *Coventry Evening Telegraph* among others. The only exception in a generally accurate record was the survey of the Falmouth constituency in 1966, but this differed from the other constituency surveys in two ways: it was carried out a month before election day and quota sampling was employed. By-election predictions since then have been notably successful. Its political polling is based upon the principle of random sampling, while its market research is more the preserve of quota sampling. It is unusual in normally including Northern Ireland in its surveys.

Opinion Research Centre was started, with Conservative Central Office encouragement, in 1966 by T. F. Thompson, previously political editor and assistant editor of the *Daily Mail*, and Humphrey Taylor, a director of National Opinion Polls. The Company, which is wholly owned by its founders, has grown rapidly so that less than ten per cent of its time and money is now spent on political polling. Since May 1967 a predictive poll has been published every month, but 1970 was its first predicted general election result. Its findings were published in the *Sunday Times* (random sample) and also in the *Evening Standard* (quota sampling) as well as in several provincial newspapers, so that the company can probably boast that the circulation of its syndicated poll is substantially bigger than that of any other organization. Other clients include the BBC, ITA, journals like *New Society*, many commercial companies and some academics. Occasionally, it undertakes a major piece of social research, such as its 1968 survey on religion in Great Britain.

The sixth poll is the Lou Harris Poll in the *Daily Express*. This, the newest Poll on the British scene, began the regular publication of its finding in September 1969. Before then, the *Daily Express* had run its own poll. The special nature of that poll was not the mystery which seemed to surround its procedures (although it *was* shy of taking the initiative in describing them), but the infrequency with which it functioned. Essentially, it was only brought into action when required by the editorial staff, at the time of a general election and particularly important local elections, or when the editors wanted figures about the public's views on the issue of the moment. Except for 1966, its predictions were very accurate, but in comparison to the other major polling organizations the relative lack of experience and statistical expertise on the part of its directors was notable and the distrust of its own findings represented an attitude unlikely to be found at either Gallup or NOP. Quota sampling was used, about 3,000 interviews were made, and there was a more than usually rigorous degree of interviewer supervision. With the advent of the Lou Harris Poll, however, much has changed. The Company, Louis Harris (Research) Ltd, is owned jointly by the American Company Louis Harris and Associates, Beaverbrook Newspapers, and Opinion Research Centre, which is the major, but still a minority, shareholder. Intended mainly as a readership and media research organization, its monthly surveys are based upon a stratified random sample in 120 constituencies of about 3,000 electors. It has been concentrating particularly on the new young voters enfranchised under the Representation of the People (1968) Act. The first survey was conducted by interviewers normally working for ORC, but since October 1969 the Mary Agar Field Services have provided the necessary interviewers.

There was a time when doubts were raised about the independence of the polls on the grounds that their personnel, both statisticians and interviewers, overlapped (Butler and Rose, 1960). It cannot be denied that there were connections between organizations. Each new company has owed something to its predecessors. The Lou Harris Poll, as has been pointed out, employed ORC interviewers for its initial survey and remains partly owned by ORC. Both Thompson and Taylor are on its Board. There are also links between many of the top managers. Henry Durant and Michael Shields were colleagues before Shields moved to direct NOP's political work. Working with him there was Humphrey Taylor who later formed ORC and became the major shareholder in Lou Harris (Research) Ltd. That Company's director, Neville Bartram, had himself worked with Taylor at NOP. This sort of link could be multiplied further. Derek Radford of Marplan, for example, has trained some of the statisticians working in other polling organizations. Nevertheless, within a short period from its foundation, each organization has become wholly independent and personal friendships continue alongside the friendly rivalry to be expected between organizations involved in the same, much publicized, business.

An introduction to sampling: random and quota

The pollsters' concept of public opinion is above all quantitative. Gallup quotes with approval Bryce's definition that it is 'the aggregate of the views men hold regarding matters that affect or interest the community'. The polling organizations, however, cannot search out every member of the electorate to ask them their opinions and then aggregate all the answers. That would take far too long and would be prohibitively expensive. They ask instead only a small proportion of the electorate and, as a result of this sample's answers, they claim to tell us what the whole electorate is thinking. 'The figures,' George Gallup has written, 'can be interpreted as a forecast of the division of opinion which would result if the same question was put to the entire electorate in a nationwide plebiscite or referendum' (Gallup, 1948, 69). In other words, polls attempt to estimate the whole from a knowledge of the part. For example, Table 1, which records the findings of a poll conducted by Gallup in February 1969, purports to show that 61 per cent of the British electorate then disapproved of the Labour Government's record. The whole electorate was not questioned, but only a part of it. To generalize from the smaller sample to the larger whole implies that the sample is a microcosm of that whole, in the same way that one drop of blood can enable a doctor to tell a man's blood group.

But people are not as undifferentiated as drops of blood. Since the part is not the same as the whole, samples inevitably exclude a very

Table 1 *Gallup Poll of February 1969*

'Do you approve or disapprove of the
Government's record to date?'

Approve	22 per cent
Disapprove	61 per cent
Don't know	17 per cent

large proportion of the population and the possibility of drawing erroneous conclusions about the whole merely from those in the sample must be obvious. Nevertheless, the mathematical theories of probability have helped us to be remarkably precise about the extent to which the findings of surveys can be used with confidence to tell us something about whole populations. This is not the place to embark upon an exposition on sampling theory; it would take too long. Besides, there are already a number of excellent books on the subject. (Moser, 1958; Conway, 1967; Cochran, 1963; Yates, 1960.) However, there are a number of simple observations which may usefully be made. All statements deriving from polls are probability statements; that is to say, they do not pretend to be completely accurate, even if such a thing were humanly possible. Although they accept the possibility of error, they nevertheless claim a high level of precision. How high is this level of precision? One obvious difficulty in answering this question is that most surveys are undertaken to estimate particular attitudes or behaviour patterns precisely because we do *not* know the answer; thus, we have nothing authoritative with which to check the level of their accuracy. If we *knew* how many electors disapproved of the Government's record, there would be little point in carrying out a survey to discover how many! Nevertheless, the accuracy which we should expect can in fact be calculated, since it is possible to estimate mathematically to what extent our sample is likely to deviate from being truly representative of the whole. Strictly speaking, the findings of sample surveys are estimates and should properly be presented in this sort of form (it is, of course, too clumsy to do so all the time): the pollster is 95 per cent certain that the proportion of the population holding opinion *x* lies between 59 per cent and 63 per cent. The extent of the deviation to be expected between the survey results and the 'real' facts depends upon three things, the size of the sample, the method by which the sample is selected, and the heterogeneity of the population being sampled.

Obviously, if we polled every elector (and every elector responded truthfully), we could be certain that our findings, within the limits of human errors of calculation and recording, represented the public opinions of all the electors. But this does not mean that very large samples are always to be preferred to smaller samples. The American Presidential Election of 1936 provides a fine and famous example of this point. The *Literary Digest* took an enormous sample of ten million individuals in an attempt to predict the victor in the November elections. Only a little more than a fifth of these returned their ballots, yet even these totalled over two million. Nevertheless, the project was nothing less than a monumental fiasco, for the prediction was wildly inaccurate. The sample, although mammoth by normal standards, was not a microcosm of the whole. The individuals had been mainly chosen from telephone directories which automatically excluded poorer sections of the electorate; in addition, it is reasonable to suppose that the twenty per cent who did return their ballots came predominantly from the more educated sections of society. Dr Gallup, on the other hand, with a sample of only a few thousand, succeeded in interviewing a cross-section of the American electorate and correctly forecast that Franklin Roosevelt would be victorious.

At the other extreme, too small a sample will produce equally inaccurate results. If we wanted to know where Englishmen spent their summer holidays we would need a very large sample indeed to include even one example of some of the moderately popular resorts. When replies can be spread out over so many possibilities and each individual category is itself small, the accuracy of anything other than very large samples must remain in doubt. Opinion polls, as a rule, prepare very broad categories and thus the probability of catching the 'right' number of respondents for each category is high. When the categories are narrow, for example, the Nationalists or even the Liberals in predictive polls, the level of accuracy to be expected declines. Thus, there is no simple rule about the best size for a sample. Each subject under study requires a separate rule. What can be said is that the ideal size depends very much on the number of possible answers available and the variety within the population under study. A sample of 2,000 is perfectly adequate for predicting voting behaviour in Great Britain, since the choices open to respondents are limited and the heterogeneity of the electorate at present slight. A by-election requires a sample of about the same size; for although attention may be limited to one out of 630 constituencies, the vital variables are not significantly reduced. The number of possible replies are certainly no fewer (they may well, in fact, be increased) and the heterogeneity of the population is only marginally decreased.

This serves to emphasize the point that polls are concerned with aggregates, with proportions of a whole population holding a particular view, not with individuals. The man interviewed on the Clapham omnibus is indeed a unique individual, but his responses are the same as 15,000 other faceless men and women might make. For each question taken separately we may conceive of him speaking for 15,000 others; but it will be a different 15,000 for each question. Yet doubts must still arise whether our sample of 2,000 individuals does in fact represent a microcosm of the aggregate of the whole population. Obviously, the failure to obtain a sample which accorded with the numerical strength of various strata within the population accounted for the *Literary Digest*'s disaster.

There has been much debate about the comparative advantages and disadvantages of random and quota sampling as a means of choosing an ideal cross-section of the nation. For the statisticians there can be no doubts; random samples are always to be preferred. In the first place, the margin of error to be anticipated can be calculated and the probability of getting a representative cross-section of the population is high. Random sampling, let it be said, is not haphazard at all but highly scientific. In a random sample, each individual within the population being sampled has a calculable probability of being selected. Indeed, the term 'random sampling' is often replaced by the more descriptive term 'probability sampling'. The population to be sampled is arranged in such a way that any bias in selection is avoided; this may be done by giving each individual a numbered disc and then selecting the sample blindfold from a turning barrel, for example, or, more simple and common, listing the population in alphabetical order and then selecting every *n*th name. The named individuals, and no one else, are then interviewed. In this way, people from every stratum get selected in the correct proportion, there can be no unconscious bias in the procedure for selecting respondents, and the extent of any probable sampling error can be calculated. In a national sample of 2,000 we should allow for an error of between one or two per cent due specifically to the sampling procedure. Any prediction which falls within this range of plus or minus two per cent must be seen as accurate polling.

In fact, no polling organization uses a 'pure' model of random sampling for its national surveys. Most use a form of what is called stratified random sampling. The population is thought of as being composed of various strata, or sub-populations, according to sex, socio-economic status, locality, religion, and so on. A stratified random sample divides the population into sub-populations and then follows the random procedure already outlined for the selection of individuals within the sub-populations. A good example of this process is provided by the system used by NOP.

The method employed to select a sample for a national survey is as follows. First, the country is divided into ten Standard Regions, the Registrar-General's nine in England and Wales, and one for Scotland. Within each of these geographical sub-populations, the constituencies are listed according to two further variables, the type of constituency and the partisanship of the constituency. Thus, the second stage of the sampling procedure is to list the constituencies within each Standard Region according to four further criteria, constituencies in conurbations, other constituencies consisting entirely of urban administrative areas, constituencies in which more than fifty per cent of the population live in urban administrative areas, and constituencies in which more than fifty per cent of the population live in rural administrative areas. This final category in fact contains many variations, since constituencies designated 'rural' can include mining and urban over-spill areas as well as genuinely agricultural districts. The third stage is to arrange the constituencies of each type according to the ratio of Conservative to Labour votes cast in the last General Election. The end product is a list of constituencies, not arranged alphabetically or being swirled around inside some revolving barrel, but ordered according to other acknowledged criteria. It is at this point that the random element is introduced. A random starting point is taken and every *n*th constituency thereafter selected for attention, until two hundred constituencies are chosen. This somewhat complicated procedure ensures that the sample is representative of all constituencies in Great Britain while retaining the methodological assumption that every constituency has an equal chance initially of being contained in the sample. Within each selected constituency interviews are carried out with twenty electors, drawn by a process of random selection from the electoral register. This procedure is statistically the soundest method of ensuring that the sample is indeed a microcosm of the whole population; the initial stratification, by accounting for the possible effects of geographical heterogeneity, in fact increases the precision to be expected (Moser, 1958, 80). The pollsters sometimes employ more detailed forms of stratification than this in their sample selection. However, since there has been a considerable movement of statisticians from one organization to another over the last decade, it would be wrong to suggest that any one company has a monopoly of virtue in this respect. Generally speaking, the nature of the stratification depends upon the object of the survey; predictive polling involves less complicated procedures than some other forms of social research.

The advantages of random sampling depend very much on the statistical arguments. Its most attractive feature is that only the named individuals selected by the random procedure may be interviewed. On the other hand, it is expensive. For one thing, the selected individuals may be dispersed over the constituency and it may require two or three visits to contact them. For another, the actual choosing of the sample takes some time and must be done anew for each survey. There is also another disadvantage: there are some people, the young and active, whom it is often impossible to contact at home. Such people may therefore elude the pollsters. It is this weakness which may account for the general under-representation of Liberals in the random surveys. Actually pollsters have consistently underestimated Liberal support, on average since 1955 by about 1·4 per cent on the last poll before a general election. This figure may not seem very significant (it is well within the acceptable margin of error) but it does represent, on average, nearly one-fifth of the total Liberal vote.

The major difference between random and quota sampling is in the process of selecting the individuals to be interviewed. The first stage of stratification, the choice of constituencies for example, is usually common to both methods. But the way of obtaining a representative cross-section of the population is not. A quota sample is selected within a constituency in the following way. First of all, the pollster discovers from census returns and other published statistics how many people in any administrative unit are men, are of a given age, or work in a particular occupation. An interviewer is then instructed to contact respondents whose composition in terms of sex, age, and socio-economic status mirrors that of the constituency itself. The detailed breakdown of the required social characteristics, as represented by Table 2, provides the interviewer's 'quota'. Since administrative units do not always coincide with constituency boundaries, the social characteristics of those interviewed in any one constituency may not, in fact, be quite representative of that constituency. Nevertheless, when all the 'quotas' are completed and the results aggregated, the end product should be a representative sample of the country. In fact, to select twenty individuals to fit the pattern outlined in Table 2 presents considerable problems. Gallup therefore simplify the task of their interviewers by giving them very general instructions. They are to choose an equal number of men and women, spread over all

Table 2   *Hypothetical scheme of quotas for 20 interviews*

Sex	No.	Age	No.	Socio-economic Status	No.
Male	9	20–29	4	Highest	2
		30–44	6		
Female	11	45–64	7	Middle	4
		65+	3		
				Lowest	14
Total	20	Total	20	Total	20

class groups and all age groups of which two-thirds must be manual workers or the wives of manual workers. If necessary, the resulting sample is corrected statistically so that it actually mirrors the age and class distribution of the constituency.

But, for a number of important reasons, the final sample may not actually be representative. The principle of quota sampling assumes that the fundamental variables are sex, age, and socio-economic status. This is not unreasonable, but it *is* an assumption. That these are not necessarily the fundamental variables, a point of view which George Gallup found difficult to recognize, is suggested by the importance of religion as an independent basis for political behaviour in the United States (Johnson, 1962). Second, the choice of actual respondents is left to the interviewer, so that in any given constituency different interviewers, while sticking to the secondary stratification contained in their quota categories, might yet select markedly different people to interview. The definition of social class is very far from exact. There is an element of truth in Alan Watkins's comment that the ideal Gallup interviewer 'must have the nose for financial standing of a bank manager, together with the obsessive interest in social distinctions of a Betjeman'. It is not difficult to imagine an interviewer, searching for a male old-age pensioner from the highest socio-economic class to complete her quota, in fact choosing as the last resort a man from the so-called, and very inexact, middle class. Third, since the interviews are usually carried out in the street or at the workplace, the elderly and infirm may be disproportionately ignored. Moser and Stuart did find that quota sampling resulted in a maldistribution in respondents' occupations and in their level of education when compared with the actual distribution in the population. Random sampling was far more representative (Moser and Stuart, 1953). It was noticeable in 1966 that the active population was over-represented in Gallup's quota sample and this showed itself marginally in the better standing of the Liberals. Thus, the spread *within* a control group may be unrepresentative, for the interviewer may well shun extremes. The importance of the interviewer, a source of bias under any circumstances, is exaggerated. Finally, the element of randomness, and thus the possibility of calculating the sample error, is abandoned.

Nevertheless, the system does have distinct advantages. It is much cheaper. Travelling is kept to a minimum; there are no call-backs; it is easier to administer since the same scheme of quotas will suffice for each survey. When there are no convenient sampling frames, like electoral registers, it may in fact be the only possible method. Generally speaking, statisticians have criticized quota sampling for its theoretical inadequacies, which cannot be ignored; market researchers and the Gallup Poll, on the other hand, defend it not merely because it is cheaper and administratively more convenient, but above all because it produces excellent results. In fact, Gallup's predictions based upon quota sampling have been more accurate than those based upon random sampling.

The final predictions of the polling organizations, which are set out on page 25, do not differ significantly, except in special cases such as Research Services' attempt in 1951 and that of the *Daily Express* in 1966. In 1970 and between elections the congruence has been much less. During the 1964 campaign NOP using random samples and Gallup using quota samples diverged considerably, not only in the size of the gap between the parties but also in the direction that the gap was moving. And this has been the case even within one organization; for Gallup carried out their predictive surveys in 1964 using both methods of sampling, and the results are presented in Table 3. The differences are unsystematic, each method favouring Labour at different times. Hence, one cannot make allowances for a permanent bias in any one direction (NOP's random sample, for instance, agreed with Gallup's quota figures in September). Before the 1964 election NOP had been consistently more favourable to the Conservatives than Gallup, but during 1965 the opposite was the case. Divergencies occur even when the same sampling procedures are used, as was exemplified most dramatically in July 1963. On the 25th NOP indicated a Labour lead of eight per cent, which represented a *fall* of ten per cent as compared with its June figures; on the following day, Gallup showed Labour leading by twenty per cent, an increase of six per cent. At this time, it should be remembered, both organizations were using quota samples. The same kind of fluctuations

Table 3   *Percentage Labour lead, February–September 1964*

	Quota	Random
February	19	12·5
March	8	8·5
April	12	6·5
May	13·5	12
June	10	10
July	9·5	7·5
August	7	10
September	0·5	4

appeared in 1969 again, although it was the extent of the movement rather than the direction which was noticeable.

What, then, are we to make of these figures? There are two basic points. First, these predictions are only probability statements and must, as has already been pointed out, be thought of as approximations to within four or six per cent. Anything which falls within that range is pretty good polling, and variations within it are due as much to chance as to skill. A single percentage point really carries no significance, so that those newspapers which suggest that a Prime Minister's popularity has in reality diminished when his rating drops by one per cent betray ignorance of the statistical foundations of the polls. Second, the predictive polls carried out immediately before a general election differ markedly from other, mid-term polls. For one thing, the care and effort expended by the pollsters during a general election campaign is greater than at other times; their rewards, both in terms of finance and publicity, encourage this; Gallup, for example, interviewed only 936 electors for their March 1969 predictive poll, instead of the 2,000 or so which they normally interview nearer a general election. For another, as is explained in the next chapter, what are being measured, voting intentions on a specific and known day, are easier to manage and calculate than mid-term predictive polls. Of course, for most of the time the major polling organizations are in harmony, but the occasions on which they so noticeably diverge may be explained by a combination of the factors just outlined. Between elections, the heterogeneity of the country is expressed more readily than during the weeks immediately before a general election; for that reason, the statistically sounder method, the random sample, should probably be followed. It is doubtful whether there is really much to be gained by merely averaging out the findings of the major polls (Leonard, 1968, 136). But when it comes to an actual general election, however, there is nothing to choose between the methods.

Miscellaneous survey problems

The fundamental problem of all surveys is the statistical one of selecting the sample. But there are a number of other sources of error which deserve mention. It would be as well to consult some of the text-books for the more refined arguments on these, for all I have done is to list the major problems which every survey faces and which most reputable pollsters largely overcome.

First, there are some people in the original sample from whom no response is forthcoming, either because they are too infirm to co-operate in an interview, or because they are away on holiday or otherwise unable to be contacted even after two or three recalls. In addition, some may refuse to answer questions at all, but this category is very small; on average it may account for four per cent of the sample (sometimes it is down to even less than one per cent and occasionally it rises to as much as eight per cent). For the most part, however, people seem to be flattered that their opinions are thought to be worthy of notice and are only too eager to express themselves on any and every topic. On average the pollsters achieve an 85 per cent success rate outside Greater London. Within the Greater London area, however, the response rate is significantly lower and the refusal rate noticeably higher, mainly because this area is the most convenient hunting ground for market researchers interested in housewives' reactions to new commodities, and householders there are thus plagued by doorstep men more than anywhere else in the country. The extent to which non-response affects the reliability of survey results depends, as we would expect, upon its magnitude and, much more important, upon the degree to which non-respondents differ in kind from re-spondents. Quota samples take no account of non-response; random samples, because the individuals to be interviewed are explicitly named, must do so. The organizations usually select a sample in excess of the number actually required so that the exact number of interviews wanted can be undertaken. Since contact is not made with non-respondents, it is difficult to say whether they differ in kind from respondents; the probability is that they do only to the extent that they are younger and more mobile than the rest of the electorate.

Second, there is the fear that respondents do not in fact tell the truth. However, the evidence of general election predictions suggests that there is a very close correspondence, despite the tradition that the ballot box should be secret, between stated voting intentions and actual voting behaviour, as is shown in Table 4. It is possible, of course, that deceivers are equally divided between the major parties and thus cancel each other out. And there are a few occasions, especially where emotions are high, when doubts may legitimately be raised, as, for example, in the Leyton by-election of January 1965. The pollsters' predictions that Mr Patrick Gordon Walker would retain his seat for the Labour Party were proved wrong. NOP returned immediately to the scene of their failure in an attempt to discover the reasons for the massive abstentions of normally loyal Labour supporters. The first question, asking why respondents had abstained, elicited the answer that less than ten per cent had abstained because of Mr Gordon Walker's stand on the immigration issue. The second question, however, asked why respondents thought the *others* had abstained and found that more than fifty per cent were thought to have done so because of the immigration issue. To what extent did these respondents hide their real motives at first and project them on to their fellow abstainers later—if at all? What evidence there is, and by its very nature it is not easy to gather, suggests that in normal situations very few people consciously mislead interviewers.

Third, the wording of a question, if it is not as neutral as possible, may give rise to bias. I shall return to this vital aspect of polling in Chapter 4 but two questions from a recent Gallup political survey can serve as illustrations of the sort of interpretive problems indifferent question design can raise. The first question was: 'If the Government decided not to apply for membership of the Common Market, would you approve or disapprove of this decision?' Thirty-nine per cent said they would approve not joining, thirty-two per cent said they would disapprove. The second question was: 'If the Government were to decide that Britain's interests would best be served by joining the European Common Market, would you approve or disapprove?' In this case, forty-three per cent were in favour of a governmental decision to join the Common Market, and thirty per cent were opposed. Interpretation of these mutually contradictory statistics is not easy. One explanation would point out that the phrase 'Britain's interests would best be served' in the second question was not neutral; on the contrary, it positively discouraged many people from disapproving what had been implicitly designated as right for their own country. Or, again, it may be natural for people unaware of and uninvolved in issues of some complexity to support govern-

Table 4   *General election forecasts 1945–66*

Extent of error

Actual %		Gallup	Daily Express	Research Services	NOP
1945					
Con	39·5	+1·5			
Lab	49·0	−2·0			
Lib	9·2	+1·3			
1950					
Con	43·1	+0·4	+1·4		
Lab	46·8	−1·8	−2·8		
Lib	9·3	+1·2	+1·7		
1951					
Con	47·8	+1·7	+ ·22	+2·2	
Lab	49·3	−2·3	−3·3	−6·3	
Lib	2·6	+0·4	+0·9	+4·1*	
1955					
Con	49·3	+1·7	+1·9		
Lab	47·3	+0·2	−0·1		
Lib	2·8	−1·3	−0·6		
1959					
Con	48·8	−0·3	+0·3		−0·8
Lab	44·6	+1·9	+0·8		−0·5
Lib	6·1	−1·6	−1·1		+2·4*
1964					
Con	42·9	+1·6	+1·6	+2·1	+1·4
Lab	44·8	+1·2	−1·1	+1·2	+2·6
Lib	11·4	−2·9	−0·3	−2·4	−2·5
1966					
Con	41·4	−1·4	−4·0	+0·2	+0·2
Lab	48·7	+2·3	+5·9	+1·0	+1·9
Lib	8·6	−0·6	+0·9	−0·3	−1·2

Note: These forecasts are the polls' final predictions and refer to Great Britain only. The don't knows and others have been excluded. The fieldwork upon which the polls are based is usually carried out at least two days before election day. For 1970 figures, see Table A in Introduction.

* = including others

ment policy, however hypothetical and inconstant. This serves to illustrate the difficulty of interpreting many opinion polls. Essentially questions must be specific if anything other than a general attitude is wanted, couched in simple language (some of the pollsters' questions are inordinately long and complicated), unambiguous and devoid of leading words.

Fourth, the face-to-face confrontation between interviewer and interviewee may be the cause of bias in two ways. On the one hand, interviewers can just make careless mistakes; if this is the case, their errors tend to cancel one another out on average, leaving little or no net error. This appears to be the most common source of bias. In earlier days, some interviewers were in effect common property, but now most organizations have their own panel of interviewers, almost all self-employed and part-time. The number of interviewers on their panels depends upon the total quantity of survey work undertaken. Marplan has about 1,000, NOP just under 900, Gallup about 800, and ORC more than 400. The Lou Harris poll employs an agency to undertake its interviewing. Before being employed, of course, prospective interviewers require some instruction in their work; the extent to which they are trained differs from organization to organization. Gallup, for example, believe strongly that the best training is experience. But all of them supervise their interviewers regularly and, since the supply of potential interviewers seems to exceed the demand, they are not afraid to dispense with the services of unsatisfactory workers. The other source of bias is more serious. For interviewers may cause non-compensating errors by so dominating the interview that the respondent offers the kind of opinion which he thinks is expected of him. This dominance may be obvious (but no organization employs hectoring interviewers for long) or subtle, where middle-class interviewers, for example, call forth middle-class responses, especially from those who do not in fact hold an opinion but feel that they ought to. This has been suggested as a reason for the comparatively pro-Conservative findings of NOP in 1964 (Pickles, 1965). The NOP interviewers were indeed more middle-class and more feminine than Gallup's, but the figures for 1965, when NOP showed a pro-Labour bias, seem to deny that this had any long-term effect. But voting intentions differ significantly from expressions of opinion, so that the 1965 figures do not dispose of the possibility that some responses, say to a question on race relations, are indicative more of the respondent's estimation of the interviewer's attitude than the respondent's own opinion. The difficulty is that interviewing can be a complicated procedure and social representativeness among interviewers would almost certainly lead to inefficiencies and inaccuracies; to my knowledge no organization employs coloured interviewers.

Fifth, the actual timing of questions involves certain problems. As far as predictive polls are concerned, there is necessarily a gap between the fieldwork of the final survey and the election day itself. These last-minute shifts of opinion are immeasurable. The 1948 Presidential election in the United States provides the most celebrated example of this, but there are many others, particularly constituency and by-election surveys in Great Britain, which fail to account for those who make up their minds after the last polling has been carried out. Another problem related to timing arises out of the decision-making process within the polling organizations themselves. Inevitably the question arises about the topics on which the public's opinions are to be sought and, almost as inevitably, the topics are those which are in the news: British Summer Time when a child is killed on his way to school on a dark morning, Northern Ireland when peace gives way to violence, ministerial popularity following ministerial pronouncements, and so on. It is right that this sort of question should be asked, but interpreting the answers is difficult. To what extent has the child or the violence affected the respondent's answer to a question concerned with generalities? Would they be the same three weeks later, or in the summer when the mornings are bright, peace reigns in Northern Ireland and the Minister at Juan-les-Pins?

All these problems are sources of bias, and thus potential error, in a survey. Many of them cancel each other out, but nevertheless there is an incalculable residual left to cause everyone a certain hesitancy in accepting the exactitude of every poll. But, when all is said and done, most of these problems can with care be largely overcome; in any case, the results of the predictive polls have generally been so accurate that we must accept their statistical reliability, if not the interpretations of them. The margin of error to be expected on any one statistic is about two or three per cent and until 1970 neither Gallup nor NOP had been outside this acceptable margin of error. The margin of error on the *gap* between the parties is twice this size, since both the Conservative figure and the Labour figure are liable to a margin of error. It should be remembered that these small errors are sufficient to mispredict an election in the United Kingdom where the parties are evenly matched. For most purposes, however, we can anticipate from the pollsters a sufficiently accurate representation of public opinion.

'Don't knows' and the presentation of polls

When a survey is completed, one policy decision that has to be taken by the pollsters is the method of presenting the 'Don't knows'. There are at least three ways of doing this, as Table 5 illustrates. Table 5A tabulates the responses to the basic question about voting intention. But this raises the question whether the answer 'don't know' implies that the respondent is genuinely in doubt but will decide

Table 5   *Gallup's method of dealing with 'don't knows'*

A   'If there was a general election tomorrow, which party would you support?'

Conservative	43	
Labour	26·5	
Liberal	7	Gap = 16·5
Other	2·5	
Don't know	21	

B   Those who reply 'don't know' get redistributed accordingly to replies to the question 'For which party would you be most inclined to vote?'

Conservative	47	
Labour	29·5	
Liberal	9	Gap = 17·5
Other	3	
Don't know	11·5	

C   Table 5B is recalculated to exclude those who still reply 'don't know'.

Conservative	53	
Labour	33·5	
Liberal	10	Gap = 19·5
Other	3·5	

later, that he is uninterested and will neither make a decision nor cast a vote, that he has made up his mind but will not inform the interviewer on the grounds that the ballot should be secret, or that he would, like the anarchists, prefer to answer 'none'. Some of these difficulties can be resolved by probing further, by pressing the respondent with another question as in 5B, for it cannot be assumed that the undecided will split evenly between the parties. In fact, evidence from post-election polls suggests that 'don't knows' almost always divide unevenly. This further probing has two interesting results in the example; it produces an increased percentage lead for the Conservatives (if the 'don't knows' had divided differently, the lead might have been cut) and it raises the Liberals' putative share of the vote disproportionately, thus indicating, perhaps, that to vote Liberal is mainly a way of avoiding voting either Conservative or Labour. Finally, since those who still express no preference after further probing are assumed not to be going to vote at all, the figures from 5B are reformulated as a percentage of those who are expected to vote. After all, the excluded are assumed to be non-voters and pollsters aim to predict the division of votes which *are* cast.

All this discussion presupposes that people who indicate, even hesitantly, that they will vote actually do so. At first sight this does not appear to be the case. For the proportion of the electorate which does not vote, 24·2 per cent in 1966, is substantially higher than the 'don't knows' even of category 5A, which were then running at seventeen per cent. However, a certain proportion of the electorate is in no position either to vote or to be interviewed; some may have died, others will have emigrated, and many more will have moved house without making arrangements for voting either in their old constituency or a new one. The exact number of this group depends on the freshness of the register; in an October election, the maximum turnout to be expected is probably just over 90 per cent. The 'don't knows' in Table 5B, therefore, seem to represent pretty accurately those who are in a position to cast a vote but will not in fact do so. This fits well with Abrams's finding that about 10 per cent of the electorate does not participate at all in political matters (Abrams, 1962). General Elections involve virtually all those who participate in politics so that the pollsters can be moderately certain that those who express preferences will act accordingly. (Some of the errors in the 1966 predictions may be accounted for by the fact that some acknowledged Labour voters in safe Labour seats did not vote.) Participation at by-elections is much lower; many who express preferences in fact abstain. This makes predictions especially difficult, particularly, as seems to have happened for the most part since 1967, when one party has suffered disproportionately from this tendency. The greater the number of 'don't knows', as we would expect from our general discussion on sampling, the greater the theoretical margin of error.

DPOP

Care must be taken when reading the published predictive polls to be certain which figures are being presented. During the 1966 election campaign the Gallup Poll 'don't knows' averaged, over five surveys, 16·8 per cent, NOP's at 3·45 per cent. The Gallup Poll was concerned with 'don't knows' in category 5A; NOP were concerned with a new category altogether, those people who said they definitely would vote but were as yet undecided for whom, a group which does not appear as a separate entity with Gallup. It is probably true to say that NOP presses its respondents harder than the other polling organizations in order to discover more accurately the underlying way in which opinions and intentions are moving. This has advantages; there are indications, for example, that NOP perceives a change of emphasis in public opinion before Gallup. On the other hand, to press too hard may anger the respondent and therefore negate much of the utility of the rest of the survey. As Table 5 shows, the figures with which party support or lead are expressed may take many forms. Should we say that the Conservatives' lead was 16·5 per cent or 19·5 per cent? If we were primarily interested in forecasting voting behaviour, we must settle for the second figure, if with popularity probably the former. In any case, we should note that under half of the electorate indicates support for the Conservative Party despite its enormous lead and the *Daily Telegraph*'s published figures of 53 per cent. These processes are peculiar to predictive polls alone; otherwise the 'don't knows' stand uncorrected. It is also relevant to point out that by formulating figures to the nearest half per cent, Gallup, along with some of the other polling organizations, introduce an additional possibility of error. If the Conservative percentage was actually 42·8 and the Labour percentage 26·7, to round the figures so that the Conservatives are seen to be supported by 43·0 per cent of the electorate and Labour by 26·5 per cent is to indicate that 120,000 more people in the country support the Conservatives than the survey in fact indicated.

The last point to make in this discussion is also concerned with presentation. Some of the comment, and most of the headlines, in the Press need to be treated with caution. Although the Gallup surveys are written up by Gallup staff and the *Daily Mail* articles on the NOP polls have to be cleared with NOP before publication, the points made are much less sophisticated than either the pollsters or students of politics would like. Editorial comment is not limited by these conventions and is accordingly more open to criticism. The surveys undertaken in Northern Ireland before the general election there in February 1969 were almost uniformly misinterpreted by the political commentators and made to sustain hypotheses they had never been intended to test. At other times, too much is read into changes of opinion which are far too small to be statistically significant; too often causal relationships are read into figures without sufficient justification; on occasions, in fact, events which have taken place after the fieldwork have been suggested as reasons for the findings of that fieldwork. In the last few years, however, comment on the polls has been more responsible. The pollsters are themselves conscious that the writing-up of their work is essentially a journalistic rather than an academic activity and this inevitably oversimplifies what are really very complex matters. Interpreting statistics is not by any means quite as straightforward as some commentators appear to think.

3

Polls and elections

As has already been pointed out, the common term Public Opinion Poll is often used to describe the findings of surveys which are not strictly concerned with opinions at all. The most publicized of these, in fact, are essentially concerned with intentions, for they attempt to predict how the public is going to vote at an election. The question pollsters ask, 'If there was an election tomorrow for which party would you vote?' is not usually concerned with an actual national election but with a hypothetical one. For only one month in every three or four years is the interviewer asking a question about an intention which can in fact be carried out soon after the response is given; these polls, conducted during the election campaigns, I have called General Election Polls. This is to distinguish them clearly from by-election polls and between-election polls. By-election polls have some of the characteristics of general election polls in that intentions can be translated into action, but they differ not only in the extent of the public being polled but in the character of the political circumstances. Between-election polls are the most numerous; they act as a sort of barometer of the public's appreciation of a particular Government and therefore seem to be concerned with opinions proper almost as much as intentions. The discussion which centres on these polls is concerned almost entirely with their relative merits as predictions of political behaviour. But it is possible that this very political behaviour may itself be affected by the publication of such predictions and this possibility, especially as represented by the hoary old problem of the bandwagon, must be considered.

General election polls

The polling organizations, as has been pointed out, spend barely five per cent of their time on political polling; they depend for their livelihood on winning contracts for market research. Some people have suggested that political polling activities may be thought of as 'loss leaders', brilliant samples of the company's ware used to entice other customers into commissioning surveys. But this is not true. They may be advertisements, but they are profitable in their own right. Polls are important to the organizations, which follow the usual practices of business enterprises in costing their products carefully, as money-spinners. They are also important as publicity, but the number of contracts the organizations win to do market research depends only marginally, if at all, upon the accuracy with which they predict election results. These predictions are, of course, the most widely publicized of their activities, but it has been said that this is in fact a disincentive to new contracts because it implies that the organizations are fully occupied. At any rate, they are very probably the least useful part of their work. George Gallup, the doyen of pollsters, has in fact written that 'all of us in the field of public opinion research regard election forecasting as one of our least important contributions' (Gallup, 1957, 21). Final predictions are published within a day or two of the General Election itself, and one can argue that there is little point in knowing approximately today what will be known accurately tomorrow.

It is this very fact, however, which places such election predictions in a specially advantageous, and far from typical, position. By the time the pollsters undertake their last survey before election day, the results of which are used to test their accuracy as predictors, most electors *know* how they are going to vote about as accurately as they know what toothpaste they use. The election date is certain; extensive publicity, on the television and radio, in the Press and on hoardings and circulars, has pressurized the elector into thinking positively about the matter; in short, by the time the last survey is undertaken he will almost certainly have come to a definite decision about how he will vote. In this case, voting intentions, although not necessarily simple decisions to make, are much more clear-cut than opinions on a current controversy. The individual knows what choices he has and knows that he is expected to make a positive decision on a specific day. A question about voting intention, especially immediately before an actual election, is therefore in a different category from a question upon an issue like the Vietnam War, on which the respondent, if he has considered the matter at all, probably has an ambivalent view.

Of course, unavoidable things may happen, like illness or a sudden demand to work overtime, to prevent the elector translating his decision into action as he would have liked. And it may also be true that some, although having taken a decision in principle, through inertia, the unpleasant weather or other competing forces, are effectively dissuaded from going to the polling booth. Others may say that they will vote in a particular way but in fact fail to do so on the day; as has already been pointed out, most polls do tend to indicate that a few more people have declared their intentions than actually vote. And finally others may genuinely make up their mind only at the very last moment, when the pollsters have completed their surveys. NOP attempted to minimize this danger in 1964 and 1966 by basing their final prediction on re-interviews with a cross-section of their earlier respondents to estimate the direction in which support was moving. It is these hazards (and no one will be caught out again quite as Gallup was in the 1948 American Presidential Election) which make polls conducted immediately prior to a general election more liable to inaccuracies than simple fact-finding surveys; the toothpaste is always there to be consulted, but the polling booth may never be reached. We should therefore expect a certain discrepancy between the pollsters' predictions and the election results. But, when all is said and done, the proximity of the election, the fact that a decision on how to vote has probably already been made, all place these predictions in a special category. By assigning the same value to each individual's alleged voting intention, pollsters are in harmony with what they are attempting to predict, since each individual's vote at the general election is potentially of equal value. Variations in constituency sizes and the number of parties competing for a seat, as any Liberal will explain, make some votes more 'valuable' than others, but this does not necessarily affect the gross figures of party support with which the pollsters deal.

But to predict the number of votes which a particular party will win is not to predict how many seats it will win. The United Kingdom is not, like the Ivory Coast, a single constituency, nor, as in West Germany, are the seats in Parliament allocated according to the proportion of votes cast for each party. To predict that forty-seven per cent of the electorate will vote Conservative is not to say how many seats the Conservative party will win. Fortunately for the pollsters, particularly since they depend more on predicting the winning party correctly than the margin of victory, the relationship between votes and seats in Great Britain is a far from haphazard one. Generally speaking, if the votes are distributed between the two parties in the ratio of A : B, the seats will be distributed in the ratio of A^3 : B^3. Thus for every one per cent of the electorate which switches from one major party to another, thirty-six seats will change hands (Butler, 1963). Behind this simple formula lie very important assumptions.

First, it is assumed that the political homogeneity of the country is such that changes are uniformly spread over the country. Second, it is assumed that the country is dominated by two political parties. Third, it is assumed that the constituency boundaries do not, as in the Republic of South Africa, discriminate against either party. All these assumptions need to be treated with some caution. Political homogeneity in the United Kingdom is expressed by the uniform nature of the swing; this has not always been so (1964, for example, provides counter-examples) nor need it always be the case in the future. There is no inevitability about homogeneity. But pollsters can guard to some extent against the problems arising from the breakdown of national homogeneity by extending their surveys to a very much larger sample of constituencies. The more heterogeneous the country, the more expensive and complicated the survey must be.

Nevertheless, the cube rule has applied remarkably well to the dominant two-party system as it functions in the United Kingdom; but this depends above all on the continuing dominance of the two parties. It would be perfectly possible, if somewhat complicated and rather less reliable, to devise a formula to deal with situations where two parties are not so dominant. And this has been quite successfully done for Canada (Qualter, 1968).

On the third point it is not always possible to take account of the bias in the electoral system caused by the unequal size of constituencies. In 1950 and 1951 it has been calculated that the Labour Party needed two per cent more of the popular vote than the Conservatives in order to win the same number of seats. This fact actually saved the pollsters many blushes in 1951. The three published polls all predicted that the Conservative Party would win the election, which in terms of seats they did. In fact, however, more people voted for the Labour Party. Had the pollsters been exactly right about their prediction of total votes, they would have predicted the wrong party as the victorious one. This consideration, taken with the fact that the pollsters do not normally survey strongly Conservative Northern Ireland, led the leader writers in 1964 to treat their findings with what turned out to be unnecessary caution. It would be possible to guard against this problem arising from the unequal size of constituencies if one knew for certain the extent of the bias; but this usually becomes clear only after the event, which is not much use for predictions. In 1966, for example, the constituencies varied enormously in size, but this did not, as in 1951, affect the application of the cube rule. The exact relationship between constituency bias and the cube rule depends upon how long constituency boundaries have remained unaltered. When they are freshly drawn and therefore reasonably equal, a bias against the Labour party appears; the longer boundaries remain unchanged, however, the less the bias seems to affect the Labour party. By 1964, in fact, it had disappeared and, if there is no redistribution before 1971, there will probably be a bias in the order of one per cent against the Conservative party.

Polls which predict general election results in Great Britain are certainly in a less complicated position than polls in many other countries where multi-partyism and heterogeneity predominate. For it is normally simple to extrapolate from the findings about prospective voting behaviour predictions about seats that will be won. This is going to become less easy if the political homogeneity of the country disintegrates or if third parties begin to play a more important role at general elections. For example, if a high proportion of disillusioned Labour voters come from very safe seats, a loss of two or three per cent of the party's share of the popular vote would affect the distributions of seats only marginally; or, if the Scottish Nationalists gathered sufficient support to win a score of Hamiltons, they would prevent the Labour Party translating thousands of votes into the expected number of seats. French elections show how multi-party systems can easily distort any simple formula for relating votes to seats. Fortunately for the polling organizations, these potential embarrassments have not yet materialized, and they can be fairly confident, even with their comparatively small samples, not only that the peculiar circumstances of a general election will help the accuracy of their predictions but also that those predictions about gross voting figures can be easily interpreted in the all-important terms of seats likely to be won by the major parties; it is, after all, seats, not votes, which determine the Government in Britain. These polls have therefore been excellent indicators of voting behaviour as Table 4 indicated. But we should remember both that the comparatively uncomplicated nature of British general elections may not endure indefinitely and that it is this very margin of error which in fact decides so many elections.

By-election and between-election polls

Once we turn our attention away from the polls conducted during general election campaigns, we become involved in a quite distinct and different political context, a context which profoundly influences both the accuracy and the meaning of the pollsters' findings. The first dissimilarity is to be found in one aspect of the peculiar nature of British representative democracy. Nowadays few people accept Burke's famous dictum that a Member of Parliament 'owes you not his industry only, but his judgement; and he betrays instead of serving you if he sacrifices it to your opinion'. Nevertheless, developments in the last century and a half have meant that the United Kingdom has become in effect one giant Burkean constituency where the Prime Minister and his Government play the part of Burke's M.P. Certainly the Nuffield electoral studies since the Second World War lend considerable weight to the view that general elections are less an aggregation of 630 separate contests and more a single, nationwide, plebiscite and it would be difficult to argue with conviction that the actions of governments in the last decade have faithfully represented the current desires of the electorate. But when a citizen participates in political affairs at times other than general elections, at by-elections or local elections, he no longer perceives his own action as being directly related to the choice of a government. Between general elections, the citizen is concerned not with the positive action of choosing between alternative élites to act as the country's government, where his focus tends to be national and long-term, but with passing judgment on the government of the day, where his focus tends to be personal and short-term.

The second major dissimilarity is this. To the man interviewed in the street between elections, there is no actual election, like death, to concentrate the mind wonderfully. In fact, a hypothetical intention is being sought; indeed, it is doubtful whether we should call it an intention at all, on the grounds that the possibility of voting may never have occurred to the respondent since the last general election. No conscious decision may have been made, for the respondent is not personally aware that there is anything to decide. In these circumstances, the famous question, 'If there were a general election tomorrow, for which party would you vote?' is really artificial and interpreting the answers consequently becomes somewhat complicated.

I shall argue here that for a significant, if small, proportion of the whole electorate these polls are merely barometers of government popularity and not necessarily a reliable indication of how people will actually vote, or not vote, when a general election takes place.

We may begin by noting that in the twilight zone between general elections, by-elections and polls have a tendency to be deceptively hostile to the government, whatever its political persuasion. They are hostile in the sense that expressions of political sentiment during the period are predominantly dissatisfied with the government; they are deceptive in the sense that those expressions of political sentiment are not reliable indicators of future behaviour when a government's very existence is at stake. The unreliability of by-election results as prognostications of general elections has been accepted for many years; and polls should be treated in the same way. A graphical representation of Gallup's predictive polls will be found to have the same pattern as a graphical representation of the parties' fortunes at by-elections (Leonard, 1968, 124, 145). Although the fit is not exact (it may differ by three or four per cent), the consistency and similarity in their patterns is remarkable. The pattern of local government election results is similar, but less so. In Reading, for example, the coincidence of local swing and Gallup poll movements is nearly perfect (R. G. Gregory, 1969, 41). At first after an election, the victorious party gains by its aura of success, but this is soon dissipated. The fact that some governments lose this aura earlier than others effectively denies that there is any iron law about the timing of this process. In the middle period, the unpopularity of the government is expressed not merely by the respondents' answers but by their actions as voters; thus, during the 1955–9 government, the Conservatives lost four seats between February 1957 and March 1958; during the 1959–64 government, they won one seat during the honeymoon period soon after the general election but lost six seats between March 1962 and May 1964. Table 6 sets out in greater detail some statistics about the polls themselves. For more than two-thirds of the period since 1947 the opposition has apparently been more popular than the government of the day. This raises some interesting questions about the democratic nature of the British political system, since it seems that the 'wrong' party is in power more often than the 'right' one. In fact, during the Conservatives' thirteen years in office, the government led only in the election years of 1955 and 1959, and in 1960 and 1961, when the Labour party was itself deeply divided. Yet only twice before 1970, in 1951 on a minority vote and in 1964 when the Conservatives lost by the narrowest of margins, had the incumbent party been defeated. By the 1959 election, the Conservatives had pulled up seventeen

Table 6:   *Gallup monthly polls*

Year	No. of months in which opposition led	monthly average of gap	largest gap	months with 8% +gap	Average % not supporting either of major parties
1947	10	3·0	11	1	24·2%
1948	12	3·5	7	0	26·7
1949	10	3·7	9	1	26·3
1950	3	1·8	3	0	19·3
1951	11	8·3	12	7	20·2
1952	12	5·2	9	1	19·3
1953	8	2·1	3	0	19·8
1954	9	1·7	5	0	19·8
1955	3	1·9	4	0	19·7
1956	11	3·0	6	0	22·4
1957	12	7·6	13	4	26·1
1958	7	4·5	10	1	29·3
1959	2	2·5	$5\frac{1}{2}$	0	24·1
1960	0	4·7	$10\frac{1}{2}$	2	26·0
1961	4	2·5	4	0	30·2
1962	11	4·5	$7\frac{1}{2}$	0	33·6
1963	12	2·3	$15\frac{1}{2}$	12	31·1
1964	10	7·3	$11\frac{1}{2}$	6	23·8
1965	5	4·8	9	1	24·1
1966	2	6·1	$15\frac{1}{2}$	4	23·4
1967	9	5·5	16	2	27·0
1968	12	16·1	$24\frac{1}{2}$	10	26·2
1969	12	12·9	20	10	31·4

percentage points from the trough of September 1957; by the 1964 election they had recovered fourteen points from their disastrous post-Profumo position in the middle of 1963. The Labour Government in 1969, although their unpopularity was more extreme and more long lasting than these examples, must have been thinking hard about the Conservative recoveries and the narrowing of the gap between the major parties from the mid-summer of 1969 suggested that a similar recovery was already materializing. For the fact is that, despite occasions when one of the major parties has held an enormous lead in the polls, the gap between the two major parties has never exceeded six per cent at a general election since 1945. In every post-war election, the party which has been leading at the polls at the dissolution has always lost support by the day of the election itself; in the last seven elections, the difference in support for the party ahead at the dissolution and the ultimate election result has averaged 3·9 per cent with a high of 9·5 per cent in 1951 and a low of 1·2 per cent in 1959. These figures can be interpreted to show that a sizeable proportion of the electorate are prepared to express their dissatisfaction with the government in one way or another between general elections but are unprepared to carry this dissatisfaction into active opposition when the very existence of the government is in doubt.

Another difference in the electorate's behaviour between elections is the regional variations. Uniformity of swing over the whole nation is one of the remarkable features of British general elections (Butler and Stokes, 1969, 135). In 1959, over sixty per cent of the constituencies fell within the range of 1·5 per cent of the median swing; while variations were somewhat greater in 1964, in 1966 once again nearly sixty per cent of the individual constituency swings were within 1·5 per cent of the median and only a handful were not within three per cent. By-elections, on the other hand, produce exceptional swings in individual constituencies, like the 23 per cent swing in Hamilton and the 22 per cent swing in Dudley, both against the government in 1967. Swings at by-elections are generally both higher than the average swing at a general election and also more varied. The average swing from Conservative to Labour in by-elections between 1955 and 1959 was 5·4 per cent (at the 1959 general election it was − 1·1); between 1959 and 1964 the average swing was 6·7 per cent (at the 1964 general election it was 2·9). On 12 June 1958, five by-elections took place and only one of them came within 1·5 per cent of the median, and that exactly at the margin. On other occasions when a number of by-elections have taken place on the same day, there has been a wide range of swings, the range itself remaining stable over the last decade. Such variations have also been discovered by the pollsters. At the end of 1967, for example, NOP found considerable differences between regions. In Scotland, there had been a small swing toward the Labour party, while the North-East showed a net swing of 15·7 per cent and the South-East one of 7·2 per cent towards the Conservatives. The swing does vary from region to region at general elections, but only by a small amount and very much less, incidentally, than the pollsters had anticipated in 1966. The small size of the samples for individual regions may account for the appearance of regional variations. Local government election results in 1969 varied regionally more than at the 1964 and 1966 general elections but somewhat less than NOP's 1967 estimation. However these statistics are viewed, the way in which net changes in political behaviour at general elections are insubstantial and evenly spread over the country, is not reproduced.

Uniform swings at general elections in fact belie the significantly increased volatility of opinion since the 1950s. The stability of the Gallup Poll findings for nearly twenty years after the war, as can be seen by looking at Table 6 again, is remarkable. With the exception of 1951 and 1957, in no year until 1963 did the gap between the parties exceed eight per cent more than twice. From the beginning of 1963, not only has the non-government party tended to lead by larger margins than previously but the movement of opinion has on occasions been exceedingly erratic. In the eighteen-month period from October 1967 to December 1969, for example, the gap between the major parties in the Gallup poll fluctuated widely, as can be seen from Table 7. It should be noted, however, that until recently Gallup averaged out the findings of two or more recent polls and this naturally dampened the fluctuations.

This volatility is indicative of the way in which irrevocable commitment to one or other of the major parties is on the wane. It may well be an indication that the number of what McKenzie and Silver have called 'secular voters' is on the increase (McKenzie and Silver, 1968). The language of politics has become much less ideological since the 1940s and this seems to have affected the electorate's perception of government. Recent surveys have repeatedly indicated that electors are more concerned with the stability of prices, the availability of housing, the opportunity of schooling, or the limitations on hire-purchase arrangements than with such topics as nationalization, modernization, free enterprise or other non-specific programmes. Consequently, the government of the day tends to be judged by many not according to the purity of its socialism, for example, but according to the price of beer and washing-machines. During Mr Wilson's second government it was almost as though any economic crisis was worth ten percentage points to the Conservatives. For example, following a comparatively successful and much publicized party conference in 1967 and an equally well stage-managed meeting with Mr Smith on board H.M.S. *Fearless*, Mr Wilson's party cut the Conservatives' lead in one month, according to NOP, from 9·2 per cent to 3·9 per cent; this recovery was borne out by a number of local council by-elections and by the party's improved showing in the Bassetlaw by-election. Soon after Bassetlaw, the government introduced new hire-purchase controls. There followed

Table 7: *Conservatives' lead over Labour in the Gallup Poll, October 1967–December 1969*

	Lead	Change from previous month
1967		
October	+5	
November	+6	(+1)
December	+16	(+10)
1968		
January	+6½	(−9½)
February	+19½	(+13)
March	+14	(−5½)
April	+21½	(+7½)
May	+24	(+2½)
June	+19½	(−4½)
July	+19½	(0)
August	+12	(−7½)
September	+10	(−2)
October	+6½	(−3½)
November	+15½	(+9)
December	+20	(+4½)
1969		
January	+17	(−3)
February	+18	(+1)
March	+16½	(−1½)
April	+16	(−½)
May	+18	(+2)
June	+13	(−5)
July	+20	(+7)
August	+11	(−9)
September	+8½	(−2½)
October	+2½	(−6)
November	+4½	(+2)
December	+10½	(+6)

an appalling performance in the New Forest by-election and a leap in the Conservatives' lead, from 6·0 per cent to 16·0 per cent in the Gallup Poll and from 3·9 per cent to 12·4 per cent according to NOP. A few months of comparative stability in the summer of 1968 showed the Conservative lead being slowly eroded, until the mini-budget in November virtually trebled it (see Table 7). Between 1959 and 1965 too, Labour's lead over the Conservatives in Gallup's predictive poll was almost perfectly matched by its lead on the question concerning the parties' handling of the economy (Butler and Stokes, 1969, 413). Despite the curious notion that two parties' handling of the economy can in fact be compared when only one of them is actually handling the economy, these figures nevertheless indicate the secular and instrumental nature of many party preferences.

These two developments, the variation and the volatility within the electorate, are two major causes of by-election predictions going astray. And certainly the accuracy of such predictions did not compare for many years with that achieved at general elections. Between October 1959 and August 1965, Gallup predicted eleven by-elections. They picked two wrong winners, and the gap between the two major parties was, on average, 7·1 per cent out. This compares with an average error of 2·9 per cent in their general election predictions. During the same period NOP predicted the results of twenty-two by-elections and selected the winners wrongly on three occasions (one, of course, being Patrick Gordon Walker's defeat at Leyton). The gap between the two leading parties was incorrectly predicted on average by 6·7 per cent; at general elections, the error had averaged out at only 2·5 per cent. The difficulty of predicting by-elections is compounded by the fact that a great number of people fail to vote; NOP's disaster at Leyton may be partly, but not wholly, accounted for in this way. In addition, the sample size used is sometimes too small to represent a cross-section of the particular constituency; the fact that a by-election takes place in only one constituency does not in fact mean that the ideal sample size will be much smaller than that used in a national survey, especially when it is remembered that people vote, or do not vote, at by-elections for a greater variety of reasons than at general elections. Individual constituency predictions have similar problems and show similarly varied results (Leonard, 1968, 175–6). In a national survey, the more extensive sample means that local peculiarities tend to cancel each other out; if they do not, they are so small in comparison to the whole sample that they affect the polls' predictive value hardly at all. Many constituencies individually differ from the polls' predictions at a general election, but in the aggregate, which concerns the pollsters, the accuracy is almost perfect. In recent years, however, the polling organizations have managed far more accurate predictions. In October 1968 NOP achieved the astonishing feat of predicting the competing parties' share of the vote in the Bassetlaw by-election to the first decimal point. Accuracy of this kind owes much to chance; but it was also the product of better techniques and this improved form continued throughout 1969.

The deceptive hostility towards the government of the day between elections can therefore be accounted for in two main ways. First of all, the artificiality of the questions asked between elections encourages many respondents to give answers which are really judgments on the government's current performance. But holding an unfavourable opinion does not entail action to express that disfavour. At a general election, it may seem more important for a traditional Labour voter to keep the Conservatives out than to punish his own party by expressing his relative dissatisfaction in the polling booth. The electors once more belong to the single giant Burkean constituency, and they perceive the choice before them in a very different way from the mid-term activity of passing judgment. Answering an interviewer, in short, involves, no irrevocable decision such as casting a vote.

Second, the diminishing degree of fixed commitment to one of the major parties among the electorate increases the possibility of volatile behaviour. It also makes any prognostications based upon between-election polls questionable; the nearer the general election, the less dubious is their value. This concept of volatility, however, is too unsophisticated to be of much use, since there is included within the totality of those who deviate from their traditional political leanings not only those who merely flirt with change but those who actually do change their allegiance. This emphasizes the importance we should attach to the degree of intensity with which an elector identifies himself with a political party.

Levels of intensity in party support

For theoretical purposes the electorate can be divided into groups with various levels of intensity in their party support. There are some who continually fail to vote under any circumstances, and these are assumed, by definition, to have no intensity of party support. Abrams estimated in 1962 that ten per cent of the electorate fell into this category (Abrams, 1962). At the first level, a sizeable proportion of electors are so loyal to their party that, even if it were to put up the proverbial pig as its candidate, they would support it unwaveringly. Neither abstention nor defection occurs to them. In 1950, Abrams calculated that thirty-five per cent of the electorate were such supporters of the Labour party and a slightly smaller proportion could be depended upon to support the Conservative Party (Abrams, 1950). Since then, however, the proportions have somewhat decreased but exact measurement is far from easy. One indication of this decrease is the larger numbers who now make up their mind for which party to vote during the last two weeks of the campaign. It doubled between 1951 and 1959. According to Gallup's figures, even in Labour's darkest days at least twenty-one per cent were prepared to admit that they would still vote Labour; in the Conservative decline, the figure was twenty-six per cent. Thus, at first sight, it would appear that nearly fifty per cent of the electorate (and this figure excludes Liberals and 'others') falls within this category. But the turn-out at by-elections is sometimes less than this figure and others besides these inveterate supporters must be included in the turn-out figures. The figures of twenty-one and twenty-six per cent, like Abrams's figures, merely represent the degree of support among the electorate below which the major parties have never dropped. It does include some voters who might in fact defect or abstain, but who at the time of the survey committed themselves to one party. (Only fifty per cent admit that, in deciding how to vote, they really sympathize with the party of their choice and do not feel that they must choose between poor alternatives.) Assuming that this includes some new converts to one or other of the two major parties, this first level probably accounts for about forty per cent of the electorate.

At the second level of intensity, some electors are prepared between general elections at least to consider defection. At by-elections, they may make a point of abstaining or even transferring their allegiance; to the pollster, they admit this transference of allegiance or acknowledge their partial defection by joining the 'Don't knows' or a minor party. A close inspection of the polls during the period of Labour's greatest unpopularity in 1968 and 1969 would show a tendency for this unpopularity to be expressed not by a switch to the other major party but by a movement towards the Liberals, Nationalists, and 'Don't knows'. But, when the general election comes, this group returns to its traditional party, for defection or abstention cannot now, when the future of the Government is in the balance, be countenanced (cf. Butler and Stokes, 1969, 40–2). The vital importance of recognizing this potential can be imagined by a glance at a poll published in the *Daily Mail* in April 1968. In this poll, 53·7 per cent of those with preferences said that they would vote Conservative if there had been an election at the time and 31·1 per cent said that they would vote Labour. But of these putative Conservative voters, only two-thirds (35·8 per cent) said that they were genuine supporters of the party, while the rest (17·9 per cent) maintained that they were just fed up with Labour. Let us suppose that this latter group were temporary defectors; if they all returned to the Labour fold at a general election, the percentage support for each party (assuming that all these voted, and nobody else did) might then be: Conservative 35·8, Labour 49·0. Quite a reversal! Of paramount interest to politicians, therefore, must be the exact size of the second level group.

Those who do not return to the fold, however, belong to the third level of intensity; for they actually defect or abstain or change from abstention to voting at a general election. These who alter their voting habits (together with the new electors and absence of those who have died or emigrated) are the people through whom governments are changed.

It should be understood that these categories are conceptual, but they can help to explain the misleading nature of between-election polls. The anti-government tradition of polls and by-elections represents in the main the temporary defection of those electors within the second level of intensity of party support. They express their dissatisfaction by abstaining or even voting against their traditional parties at by-elections and by replying to pollsters as though the question about voting intention was really a matter of judging the government's performance. The introduction of a genuine choice between potential governments at a general election drives this group back to its traditional home because to prevent the election of the rival party is more important than expressing dissatisfaction with their own. As so often is the case in politics, what matters are relative positions. In other words, when the Labour Party was twenty-two percentage points behind the Conservatives in March 1969, this did not mean that the gap between the parties, if there had been a real general election then, would actually have been twenty-two percentage points.

Of course, it would be wrong to emphasize the misleading nature of these between-election polls too much. One poll by itself may be inexact to a greater or lesser extent; but a series of finding (the question always remaining the same) will almost certainly indicate tendencies. If the two major polls agree on the tendencies they are illustrating, it can safely be assumed that that tendency does reflect the direction of whatever lasting movement of opinion there is. Yet beneath the outward signs of movement, enduring traditions exist and a politician still requires skill to be certain that the patent movement in his direction is a genuine and lasting shift of opinion linked with the third level of intensity or only an aberration on the part of second level voters, whose support for a rival party will evaporate when a general election comes. Aneurin Bevan thought that the polls took the poetry out of politics, but they have not taken away the skill of reading them aright. By-elections and between-election polls undoubtedly indicate trends and, to some extent, the stability of those trends. What must be guarded against is taking the exact percentage figures at their face value.

The 'bandwagon'

There has been some discussion, in Parliament and outside, about a further aspect of these polls. It has been suggested that some electors see which party is expected to win and then 'climb on to the bandwagon' and support that party. Henry Durant has gone on record as saying that anyone who resurrects this thesis is wasting public time; but, notwithstanding his strictures, it would be a mistake to ignore this particular debate. Statistical support for the bandwagon thesis is admittedly meagre, but it is not altogether absent. Berelson found in the United States that voting intentions were always very highly correlated with expectations as to who would win the election. But this might be due either to projection (that is assuming that the party one supports will win), or the bandwagon. 'The bandwagon effect,' he concluded, 'and the projection effect are approximately equal in strength' (Berelson et al., 1954, 289). In Britain, the best example of a possible bandwagon effect remains the Orpington by-election of 1962. NOP predicted that the Liberals would poll four per cent more votes than the Conservatives; on the day they polled nearly eighteen per cent more. One implication is that many electors only voted Liberal when it was seen that their votes would not be wasted. The rest of the evidence is more indirect. After the election of 31 March 1966, Gallup found what Henry Durant called a 'halo', ten per cent too many people saying that they had voted for the Labour Party. Milne and Mackenzie, in their study of the 1955 election in Bristol North-East, found that there was an increase in confidence in the superiority of the winning party after the election (Milne and Mackenzie, 1958, 115, 161, 202–3). It is not implausible to transfer this post-election bandwagon effect to the pre-election period and to suggest that the same kind of behaviour would show itself in some voters supporting the party tipped to win. According to this argument, there is little difference between those who want to be known as having backed the winning party and those who would be prepared, in order to ensure their having backed the winning party, to support the favourite in the polling booth. This line of reasoning seems to have affected a majority of the Speaker's Conference on Electoral Reform. The Conference decided in 1967, by a majority of nine to five, that the publication of polls or of betting odds on the likely result of a parliamentary election should be banned during the seventy-two hours preceding the close of the polling booths (Cmnd. 3275).

The Government, however, was not convinced that such publication unduly influenced electors; in addition, it felt that the Conference's proposal was impracticable since there were bound to be evasions which could not be at all easily suppressed (Cmnd. 3717). Most of the evidence in fact supports their scepticism. The phenomenon of the 'halo' is unique; it did not appear even after Labour's other great victory in 1945 (Cantril, 1951, 197). Nor did Milne and Mackenzie find increased confidence in the winning party after the 1951 election (Milne and Mackenzie, 1954, 153). Butler and King maintain that there was no evidence in either the 1964 or the 1966 elections that polls produced a bandwagon effect, essentially on the grounds that the Labour majority was *less* than any poll had suggested (Butler and King, 1965, 207; 1966, 174). Bromhead follows the same line (Bromhead, 1966, 334). Not only was the swing to Labour *less* than the polls had predicted, but the polls showed no increase in support for the Labour party during the campaign. As has already been pointed out, in every post-war election the party which has been leading in the polls at the dissolution has always lost support by the day of the general election itself. More evidence is provided by a Gallup Poll in September 1964, which found that only thirty-eight per cent of those interviewed claimed to know what at least one poll was showing. Furthermore, the level of accuracy in these people's recall was very low. Only fifteen per cent of the total sample correctly recollected who was leading in any particular poll. An NOP poll at the same time found that only ten per cent had a correct recollection. In a sense, however, this is rather unsatisfactory evidence since at the time the situation was confused by Gallup showing Labour to be leading and NOP showing the Conservatives. In the less doubtful conditions of 1966, recall was much better. After the election NOP found that fifty-three per cent of their sample claimed to have seen poll forecasts and forty-two per cent remembered that they had forecast a Labour victory. (In both cases, I suspect that some people said that they had seen the polls, but had not in fact done so.) It seems from this that, in so far as polls have any potential to create a bandwagon effect, they can only do so when one party is already a long way ahead of its rival. But those eager to discover a bandwagon effect would maintain that the twenty-five per cent or so who are aware of the polls may be the trend-setters and that we should really be thinking in terms of a three-step flow of communication, first to the news media, then to the opinion leaders, and finally to the ordinary citizen. Yet it is somewhat curious to suggest that opinion leaders are slaves of opinion polls. All these rationalizations furthermore completely ignore the incontrovertible fact that the Labour lead in the polls did *not* increase in 1966 despite their considerable lead at the beginning of the campaign. Presidential elections in the United States of America should provide further evidence of the potency of a bandwagon, since Californians still have five hours in which to vote after the first results from the Eastern seaboard begin to get broadcast. Surveys in 1968, however, indicated that the knowledge of initial trends produced no measurable impact on voting behaviour (Jowell and Hoinville, 1969).

It may nevertheless be possible to construct a theory which allows for the bandwagon to roll ever so slightly. The opinion polls published immediately before a dissolution are somewhat misleading in that they refer not to an actual general election but to a hypothetical one. At that stage, there is no general election to occupy the mind. If the concept of a second level of intensity in party support is valid, we should expect the more popular party's lead to be whittled away as many electors return to the party of their traditional allegiance. This coalescence of the two levels of intensity means that there is in any case very little room left for the bandwagon effect to occur among the remaining electors. An actual bandwagon effect, inevitably small and therefore no more important than other apparently irrational forces deciding voters' behaviour, may be hidden by a steady and larger movement (in the 1966 case of Conservative voters), returning to the party which had been losing their support during the previous months. The statistical evidence for this theory is slender, but not altogether absent. If the detailed movements of the polls in the election campaigns of 1959, 1964 and 1966 are looked at, two points do emerge. (The very slight shifts of opinion are not, strictly speaking, statistically significant in themselves, but the similarity of all the polls in these elections demands some attention.) First, there is a movement back to the underdog, indicative of second level voters returning; then, in the last days, there is a gentle bandwagon, probably from the 'don't knows', which gives the leading party a small lift just before polling day. There has, in fact, been a tendency for those who make up their minds at the very last moment to plump for the party which eventually wins (Butler and Rose, 1960, 105; Butler and King, 1965, 208; 1966, 174). Such a theory is purely conjectural. The technical problem remains that of isolating a bandwagon effect from the many more significant variables which occur in elections.

The trouble is that arguments about the effects of polls on voting behaviour can take so many forms. One could support the hypothesis that the publication of these polls encouraged the typically British support for the underdog and thus worked in the opposite direction, deserters becoming doubly determined to return to the ranks. The publication of polls may thus galvanize the back-runner and his supporters into greater effort and determination, as it has been suggested NOP's unflattering estimate of Liberal support in Orpington did in 1964 (Butler and King, 1965, 210). This is akin to the 'morale boosting' argument, which goes further than repeating the commonplace that a party's morale is raised if the polls indicate a trend in its favour. It suggests that this boost is translated into such a renewed enthusiasm for electioneering that a marginal seat or two may be won which might otherwise have been lost (Plowman, 1960). An equally plausible hypothesis might suggest that, by showing the large margin of one party's lead, that party's supporters may feel that there is little incentive to translate their own support into action at the polling booth. A kind of precedent for this would be the way in which Labour voters in safe Labour seats in the 1964 and 1966 elections, when Labour was expected to win, had a lower turn-out than the average (Butler and King, 1965, 358; 1966, 294; Bromhead, 1966, 334). A further example of this might be the Leyton by-election of January 1965. The NOP poll, published on an inside page by the *Daily Mail* under the heading 'Gordon Walker set to win', indicated a 21·7 per cent advantage to the Labour Party. It might be argued that this was a powerful disincentive to Labour supporters voting. 'How many Labour supporters,' Plowman once asked about the 1959 election, 'already struggling between conscience and apathy, looked at the poll and gave up the ghost in advance?' (Plowman, 1960). Yet, how many Labour supporters actually looked at the inside page of the *Daily Mail* in January 1965?

Polls produce overconfidence; polls produce despair. One may take one's pick. And I have no doubt that still more theories could also be advanced. Certainly, the gross changes between voting intention and voting performances are very much greater than the net changes

(Jowell and Hoinville, 1969; Butler and Stokes, 1969, 428–31). This suggests that many factors affect the fifteen to twenty per cent of the electorate who do not remain undeviating supporters of one or other of the political parties, some pressurizing the elector to support what happens to be the most popular party at the time, others pressurizing him to do the opposite. There is not, therefore, much scope for a bandwagon effect to occur. While the publication of polls may take some of the excitement out of elections (although one day the inevitable possibility of error in sampling may cause some gloriously bizarre prediction), there is no evidence to indicate that there is a causal relationship between their publication and voting behaviour. On the contrary, the very fact that the hypotheses can be so varied suggests that there is no general bandwagon effect at all, in any direction; there are both Orpingtons and Leytons. I suspect, however, that there are a majority of Californias. At the best, the thesis is unproven; certainly there is no cause for any dogmatic assertion about it. In my view, the balance of evidence is against the bandwagon thesis.

4

Polls and the public's opinions

The quantitative approach of pollsters requires that individual responses be given a simple numerical value. In its most common form, this means that 'yes' answers, 'no' answers, and 'don't know' answers are given the notional value of one. This straightforward trichotomy presents few problems of calculation; the number of answers of any one kind are added together and then expressed simply as a percentage of all those interviewed. On some issues this is an entirely appropriate way of proceeding, especially when the possible replies are strictly limited as, for example, in the question, 'Did you vote at the last general election?' Unfortunately the possible replies that can be given to most questions seeking the public's opinions are far more numerous than those that can be given to questions about facts or even intentions. First, the question arises whether some utterances which are expressed as explicit opinions are not really meaningless. Second, the questions themselves may raise legitimate doubts about the extent to which respondents have really understood them. Third, the notional value of one given to all expressions of opinion seems to ignore that opinions can be complex, many-sided, and full of reservations, so that it is not always easy for the respondents to decide exactly what their single opinion is on a topic of considerable controversy. Finally, having raised doubts about whether some answers, because they are meaningless, should be given any value at all and whether other answers, because of their complexity, should all be given the same value, we may usefully discuss some techniques designed to cope, in a simple way, with the problem of measuring the differing intensity with which opinions are held.

The problem of meaningless opinions

Once we enter the controversy of what constitutes a meaningful opinion and what does not, we are likely to be caught up in all manner of complicated semantic and philosophical arguments. Here we are not concerned primarily with the objective subject-matter of the opinion whether, for example, Guyana is actually in Africa or not, but with the subjective view of the respondent, whether he *thinks* Guyana is in Africa or not. A meaningful opinion is not the expression of a reflex reaction or a random response. Although a respondent may express an opinion devoid of intellectual motivation or based entirely upon prejudice rather than information, he expresses a meaningful opinion if he is himself aware of that opinion previous to its expression. Suppose that a survey is being conducted to discover what the British electorate's views are on the resignation of General de Gaulle as President of France. Respondent A, not quite clear who de Gaulle is and totally unaware of any views that could be held about Anglo-French relations, says that he thinks the General's departure will be good for Britain. But he expresses this definite opinion only in order to be polite to the interviewer. Respondent B, on the other hand, having built up a dislike for the General over a period of some years and having heard a television commentator's opinion that de Gaulle's going would be beneficial to Britain, answers in the same way as A. I would say that the first respondent's opinion was meaningless, while the second's was meaningful, although perhaps of dubious value. But that is altogether another problem.

One way of circumventing this difficulty would be to include in the survey only open-ended questions of this type: 'What do you think about General de Gaulle's resignation?' Respondent A would probably find it difficult to make any relevant reply. Respondent B, however, could still express with some confidence his view that the General's departure was a blessing. Even answers to open-ended questions are frequently couched in such generalities that it is impossible to decide whether they are based on anything other than a feeling that there is an obligation to respond. In any case, the diversity of replies would be such that quantification would become very complicated, since all the various answers would have first to be arranged in a small number of specific categories. Such surveys are difficult to analyse; but, more importantly, they are also more expensive than surveys in which carefully prepared answers are provided for the respondent to choose from. Public opinion polls tend not to use open-ended questions.

The implication behind every interview is that a respondent *does* have a meaningful opinion to offer. It is by no means certain that this is the case. The questionnaire may well be a catalyst forcing him to express himself on subjects about which he has no information at all and to which he has given no thought. It offers him in addition a choice of several possible answers and thus, by suggesting a distinct and limited range of choices, steers his thoughts into particular channels not of his choosing. It is a real possibility, therefore, that his answer may be selected at random from the choices presented to him, and to that extent be meaningless.

The possibility that many of those who are interviewed are similar to our respondent A is confirmed by some fascinating research carried out by the Opinion Research Center in Michigan (Converse, 1964). In 1956, a randomly selected sample of electors was asked a number of questions about their general attitude on the most suitable relationship between private enterprise and governmental activity in the economy. In order to eliminate those who genuinely held no relevant opinion, the interviewers were instructed first to read out the specific question, second, to ask the respondents whether they actually held an opinion on the topic, and only if the answer to that question was affirmative were they to go on to the third stage, that of eliciting answers to the specific question. A number of respondents admitted that they held no opinions. Despite this filter procedure, which provided an opportunity to admit that no opinion was held, the responses that were forthcoming showed remarkably low correlations with other appropriate parameters. That is to say the pattern of individual respondents' answers differed so much from what would be expected from their identification with particular political parties, their socio-economic status, or their replies to similar attitudinal questions, that the researchers began to wonder how meaningful were the results of their survey. It seemed that many people had passed through the opinion filter to record answers in a singularly haphazard manner.

The survey was repeated in an identical form in 1958. The capacity of individuals to choose the same side of a basic issue twice in succession was very low. In addition, a good many who had claimed to have no opinion in 1956 now had an opinion, while others who had claimed to hold opinions in 1956 no longer did so. Some explanation for the extent of the variations was clearly called for. Converse and his associates concluded that a considerable number of respondents passed through the filter procedure although they did not in fact hold opinions at all. Perhaps they feared to appear ignorant or to fail in their duties as citizens. This led to the suggestion that in ordinary survey work the proportion of 'don't know' responses (some of which are always to be expected) was but the tip of an iceberg representing a large proportion of citizens incapable of responding in a meaningful way. The survey was repeated once again in 1960 with the same seemingly erratic responses. This confirmed previous views. Analysis indicated that there existed a hard core of opinion on a basic, semi-ideological issue which was well crystallized and stable over time; but for the remainder of the population, response sequences were wholly random (and thus theoretically calculable). While it is acknowledged that internal logical coherence is frequently absent from an individual's general attitude towards politics and political issues, the lack of coherence in this study was so extreme that the research team concluded that only between one-fifth and one-third of the replies represented meaningful opinions. A comparable longitudinal study carried out in Britain by Butler and Stokes between 1963 and 1966 produced broadly similar response patterns (Butler and Stokes, 1969, 176–82). Only thirty-nine per cent stuck to an identical and definite position on the broad lines of nationalization policy. Although the proportion of the sample supporting entry into the Common Market was stable over time, stability in fact hid a very considerable degree of opinion change among individuals. This sort of statistics indicates the difficulty inherent in interpreting the meaning of a single set of statistics published in a newspaper.

A meaningful opinion can be defined, in the second place, in relation to the object of the survey itself. This approach is mainly concerned with problems of interpretation. For example, when some American scholars in 1958 were interested in the public's allocation of blame for the economic difficulties then apparent between a Congress controlled by Democrats and a Republican President, it was discovered that less than one-third of the public shared the primary information of divided control on which the whole survey was to be based (Converse, 1964, 21–2). The answers to the survey, if it had been undertaken, would have told us something meaningful, but it would not have told us anything useful in the particular context of allocating blame between Congress and the President. One must therefore be cautious about interpreting the findings of polls. This arises from the fact that we often expect interviewees to possess more knowledge than they in fact do. Even in a highly developed and educated country like Britain, twenty per cent of the electorate was unable to name a single party leader in the 1959 election year and, perhaps more alarmingly, twenty-eight per cent of these who claimed to be party *members* were unable to name even three of their own party leaders, let alone the leaders of any other party (Abrams, 1962, 234). It is interesting that these figures, and those of America, compare unfavourably with an underdeveloped and less literate country such as Tanzania, where voter knowledge was found to be remarkably high on basic matters (Cliffe, 1967, 278; Hyden, 1968, 226). We should not, therefore, be surprised that a high proportion of the population hold no views on the Common Market. In fact, if there is not a high 'don't know' response, there is every reason to question the findings of the survey.

The reason for this probably lies in the individual's involvement in the subject being surveyed. This was high during the 1965 election in Tanzania; it tends to be low on political matters in Britain. The average individual has no control over, or involvement in, the subject of much opinion research (like reintroducing capital punishment, entering the Common Market and so on); his opinions on these subjects are much less articulated, much less surely held, than opinions on matters within his direct experience and interest, like the quality of rival beers or the advantages accruing from various insurance policies. On the one issue, only a proportion of respondents answer from knowledge or commitment. Consequently, interpreting the meaning of the results of a survey is difficult. Perhaps we should talk of the existence of many issue publics and note that a realistic picture of opinion in the mass public is one which captures with some fidelity the fragmentation, narrowness and diversity of many publics. Perhaps the pollster's first step ought to be to ask the respondent whether he holds an opinion, whether he belongs to the issue public. But even this, as we have seen, would let through its net some who respond in a random and totally uncommitted way. By raising these questions, doubt must be cast on the pollsters' assumption that opinions can be measured as one, whoever holds them and whatever their meaning.

Questions as a source of bias

If we are to make any inferences from the polls' statistics (and this is, after all, their purpose), we must be sure that the question is interpreted by all respondents in the way which has been intended. There are at least five possible failings in the pollsters' formulation of questions which need to be considered before attempting to interpret replies with any confidence. I received the impression that the regular polling organizations gave less attention to the nuances of question design than social scientists outside the business world. This is not altogether surprising. Deciding the topics and the order in which the non-political questions should come leaves them little time to concentrate on producing wholly unambiguous questions.

First, there is the problem of leading words which was mentioned in Chapter 2. Some questions are so phrased that they strongly suggest to the respondent that a particular reply is expected. Iain Macleod made a valid point when he complained about the wording of a question used by Butler and Stokes in their study of political change in Britain (Macleod, 1969). Here is the question: 'There is quite a bit of talk these days about the different social classes. Most people say they belong either to the middle class or to the working class. Do you ever think of yourself as being in one of these classes ?' To be informed that *most* people think in this way is surely to predispose the respondent into giving an affirmative answer. It should be noted, however, that Butler and Stokes had changed the formulation of the question by their 1964 survey (Butler and Stokes, 1969, 478, 491–2).

Second, questions may be misunderstood. We are familiar with the obvious difficulties inherent in asking questions about devaluation and revaluation, or about the National Debt, or about the introduction of 'worker directors'; there will be no uniformity among respondents as to the exact nature of the subject matter. Similarly, responses themselves can be quite misleading, like the man who described himself as a bank director, on the grounds that he directed people to the appropriate cashier's counter in the bank. Words do not have identical meanings throughout the country as the Labour party discovered when preparing for the 1964 election. One of their projected slogans had unsavoury connotations in the north of England and one poster gave rise to very unfavourable comments from women while gaining the approval of men (Rose, 1967, 76, 81). All communication is liable to this kind of difficulty. And it should be remembered that opinion polls are dialogues, not monologues, so that there is always a possibility that misunderstandings will occur.

Arising from this is the third point. Simple questions are less likely to be misunderstood than lengthy, convoluted questions. Here are two questions from a Gallup survey which exemplify what should be avoided: 'Do you think it is a strength or a weakness of the Labour Government that they have a close relationship with the trade unions ? In other words, should they stress it as an advantage to be close to the trade unions or should they keep as quiet as possible about it ?' After this mouthful, the possible responses presented to the respondent were not concerned with the last part of the question – should the Labour party keep quiet about their association with the trade unions? – but with the strengths and weakness of the association. The second question also raised ancillary allusions which served to obscure, rather than illuminate, the main purpose of the question: 'Which do you prefer, to have an extra hour of daylight in the morning as we used to have when the clocks were put back to Greenwich Mean Time in the winter, or to have an extra hour of lightness in the afternoon as we have now that we keep to British Standard Time through the year?' Such excessively convoluted questions, however, are the exception, not the rule. But two-sided questions are not at all uncommon.

Like the Gaullic referendum, they in fact ask more than one thing. 'Are you satisfied with this Government and its economic policy?' is one such example; another would be: 'Do you think that unions and employers should or should not have written contracts which are legally binding, and set down such things as wages, working conditions, and productivity?' Interpreting the responses to a question of this kind is very hard. This is because some issues are so complex that respondents do not have *one* opinion on the matter but several. What could be done is to ask a number of simple questions on different aspects of, say, industrial relations, give each reply a notional value, and produce a score from the answers. The result may be thought to represent a general attitude. At the same time, however, one must be careful not to ask too many questions, for it is only the geniality of the respondent which permits interviewers to pry into what are essentially private affairs. Nor is there any point in expecting the respondent to understand the subtlest nuances which the interviewer has in mind. Too long a questionnaire, or too trivial a subject matter will produce untrustworthy results. A piece of research reported recently in *The Times* provides a perfect example of this last point. Apparently, the research indicated that 'as many as 47 per cent of those who filled in the questionnaire got their replies wrong because they did not understand the form, or were in a hurry to get rid of their interrogator, or were just having a laugh'. This is hardly surprising when the subject of the survey is discovered. To quote again, 'more than 1,000 adult Londoners were subjected to preliminary interviews in which they were asked to tabulate their feelings about five brands of headache pill in 60 scales dealing with such dichotomies as safe/dangerous, easy to swallow/hard to swallow'. It is difficult enough to name five brands of headache pill, let alone be aware of the varied properties of them all. The number of people who could conceivably be conscious of differentiating between such pills according to sixty qualitative scales must be minute. Even the survey into those who carried out surveys into the reactions to President Kennedy's death has greater value (Beck and Saravay, 1967).

There is a fourth way in which questions may introduce a bias, it can be argued, since the actual questions asked must be selected from an infinite number of possible ones. We must ask in what sense the 'right' questions are in fact asked. It is entirely possible (indeed, I would have thought probable) that the topics on which the pollsters ask questions are not in fact the topics with which the general public is most concerned. The results of the survey may be wholly representative as far as they go, but they may fail altogether to give us a realistic impression of what the public is actually thinking. It may be that, in January 1969, sixty-nine per cent of British adults did think that Trade Unionists who defied some putative anti-strike legislation should be liable to a fine. But can we therefore say that the British people were strongly in favour of anti-strike legislation? Those who found these statistics distasteful argued along two lines. First, the poll gave a selective view of what the people were actually thinking, since a more accurate representation of public opinion would indicate that industrial relations occupied the nation's thoughts far, far less than many other social, recreational, or personal issues. To obtain the true picture of public opinion would require some knowledge of people's priorities. Now, this would not be impossible. An open-ended question such as 'What problems have you been thinking about today?' might give a very different insight into what the public was really concerned about. It is only rarely that the pollsters do this. There is thus a substantial element of truth in the claim made by some congenital poll-knockets that the people are only asked for their views on issues which the pollsters, and their backers, present to them. This leads into the second aspect of the generic attack on public opinion polls. It is argued that they have policy implications from which the choice of questions cannot be divorced. Unofficial strikes was a bogus issue; the 'real' problem, the topic for the 'right' questions, was the relations between, and the comparative standard of living of, management and workers. Social scientists, particularly in these days of methodological debate, perpetually argue about the 'right' questions to ask. This is important, for the very fact of asking certain questions excludes other possible ones. It is no coincidence that most élitists discover élites, polyarchists discover polyarchies, and Marxists discover distinct economic classes. To ask questions about trade union reform, therefore, may be to give the topic a public importance out of all proportion to the importance given it privately, and to that extent public opinion has been distorted.

This distortion is closely related to the final point. Current news items dominate the questionnaires. When Captain O'Neill resigned as Prime Minister of Northern Ireland the Gallup Poll immediately drafted four questions about Northern Ireland and the Unionist Party. People may be expected to have some views on this sort of issue. Often, however, pollsters overestimate the extent of people's knowledge. For example, in the same week, the Monopolies Commission produced a report on licensing laws, and eight questions were drafted to deal with this event. It is doubtful, however, if very many people knew what the Commission had said, let alone what the implications of its report might be. Thus, it is difficult to be sure what should be made of findings that suggest that thirty-five per cent of the British people think that the Monopolies Commission's recommendations would lead to a wider choice of different brands of alcoholic drinks. The obvious reason for the pollsters' seeking out opinions on topics of this kind is that the editors of the journals in which the polls are published require statistics and stories on what they consider to be the matters of the moment. The *Daily Express* poll, when it functioned, only went into action when the editors required statistics on an issue which interested them; even now, the Lou Harris poll is guided to some extent by editorial requirements. The Marplan quarterly survey involves a set of questions on the 'issue of the moment'; what exactly the issue is going to be, for it is not self-evident, rests on the decision made by Derek Radford, the poll's director, in consultation with David Wood and William Rees-Mogg of *The Times*. Research Services only undertake political survey work for particular topics which their sponsors invite them to carry out. Gallup and NOP, however, are normally responsible for their own choice of topics. NOP did once conduct a poll of the Huyton constituency at the request of the *Daily Mail* to see whether the failure of Labour to hold either of the two local authorities in the April 1969 elections was mirrored by the electorate's preference for a replacement for Harold Wilson. Despite what the editors probably felt to be a disappointing result, the *Daily Mail* published on the front page the result that a small majority still favoured the Labour Party. The Gallup Poll's long-standing interest on the Rhodesian Question had regularly produced findings which the editorially conservative *Daily Telegraph* cannot have found to its liking. On the whole, however, the polling organizations are not so much prisoners of their sponsors as prisoners of events. What is currently newsworthy may be an intricate and many-sided matter; it is this factor above all which leads the polling organizations into asking questions the replies of which are especially hard to interpret.

Opinions and the notional value of one

Simple polls presume that all answers can quite straightforwardly be given the notional value of one, which enormously assists coding and calculation. This implies that a change of opinion springs into existence in an infinitesimal space of time, since the reply given today, however hesitantly, may be replaced tomorrow by a diametrically opposite one, given with equal hesitation. There are no half-opinions. In short, as far as the polls are concerned, either one supports the reintroduction of capital punishment with no reservations or one does not; the only other choice is to take refuge in the neutral zone of the 'don't knows'. These polls aim to present a clear-cut, boldly drawn picture, which is also static, like a single frame in a cine film. That an opinion represents a static state of affairs which is already in the past, and which has in all probability slightly altered, need cause little concern, provided that this is generally recognized. Nobody really imagines that what people said in the first week of April will necessarily be repeated in the first week of May. It may of course be useful to know from one poll what opinions people did express at the beginning of April, but it is probably more useful to discover from subsequent polls what movement of opinion there has been by the beginning of May. Polls repeated at intervals, although static calculations individually, tell a good deal as a series about trends in public opinion.

No, what is more disturbing is the clarity of focus which these snap-shot polls appear to show. Bogart, for example, has argued persuasively that, on any one given topic, people in actual fact 'hold a variety of opinions, articulated or vague, public shading into private' (Bogart 1967, 342). Thus on a general question about entry into the European Community, for instance, a person may actually hold several views, some favourable, some unfavourable. The economic arguments may be clearly articulated, the emotional and patriotic ones not so. And they are likely to differ in their expression depending upon the role the respondent is performing at the time, whether it is a public one like that of the business man or householder or a private one like that of father or husband. There is certainly a difference between public and private expressions of opinion (Harrisson, 1940). These opinions may be mutually incompatible and we are therefore

FPOP

left with the problem of deciding which, if any, constitutes the *real* opinion.

Two surveys illustrate part of this difficulty. A Stanford University poll conducted early in 1966 found that a majority of respondents supported both the administration's handling of the war in Vietnam (when the commitment was growing) and also the policy of de-escalation. Suppose, in this not untypical case, that one public opinion poll had asked the single question, 'Do you approve or disapprove of the Administration's handling of the war in Vietnam?' and another had asked the question, 'Do you approve or disapprove of a policy of de-escalation?' Which of the different answers should we accept as representative of American opinion? A similar confusion can be seen in a survey conducted by Opinion Research Centre in the summer of 1967. Forty-eight per cent of the sample agreed that 'the British Government should *enforce* one man one vote in Rhodesia *in the next two years*'; yet fifty-nine per cent of the same sample agreed that the Rhodesians 'should *get* independence under Mr Ian Smith's Government provided he agrees to *steady progress* towards African Government'. These two views are almost certainly incompatible. That eleven per cent of the sample should accept both views is an indication of the unperceived subtleties inherent in detailed questions of this kind.

The fact of the matter is that opinions are complex. Answering an opinion question, as I have already pointed out, is a very different performance from answering questions of fact ('Do you have television in this house?') and significantly different from questions of intention ('For which party are you going to vote?'). The respondent requires little or no thought to say whether he possesses a television; to express his opinion on capital punishment when asked unexpectedly by a complete stranger is altogether a different experience. The way in which the question is asked as well as the personality of the interviewer may focus the attention of the respondent on to one part of the question only. Thus, in an American example, it may well be that people with no strong views were predisposed towards expressing approval simply because the war was a national endeavour to which they felt they owed support. Similarly, the phrases 'one man, one vote' and 'African Government', although only a part of what is by no means a simple question, with its democratic overtones may have predisposed respondents to indicate agreement with the hypothetical policies. There may thus be an element of selective inattention to some of the question; in this way different answers may be due not to different attitudes but to different perceptions of what the question is really asking. Uncommitted respondents may fasten on to a particular word to guide them in their replies, so that the truth behind a respondent's reply approving the Administration's conduct of the war in Vietnam may possibly be that he has given the matter no thought; he merely accepts it, and since he does not actively disapprove of it, feels constrained to say that he approves. The catalyst of the question implying that there are two reasonable attitudes only to hold on a given issue may drive people into answering.

Given the complexity of many opinions, it is impossible in most cases to be certain that one has discovered the 'real opinion', even if such a thing could exist. This problem is compounded by an almost inevitable bias built into the polls. For instance, when the *Sunday Times* published a survey on the public's attitude to cuts in public expenditure in January 1968, it was noticeable that the third most popular reply to the open-ended question about what cuts should be made was a proposal to cut the size of the Civil Service. But this was not even an option on the list prepared by the pollsters from which respondents were later to choose. Most questionnaires have this major failing. What they do is to circumscribe the respondent to selecting, from a few limited and by no means exhaustive choices, the one answer which comes nearest to his real, often ambivalent, position on the issue (and often, of course, he has no position at all). Since there is no allowance for hedged opinions or opinions not provided for by the various possible replies written into the questionnaire, the assumption behind the polls' calculations that each response can be given the notional, but equal, value of one is not to be accepted without question. Nevertheless, while it may be true that some topics are too complicated for most respondents to grasp even the fundamentals or to express only one clear preference on, this does not mean that opinions on such topics should not be considered.

We all know that the question, 'For which party would you vote if there was a general election tomorrow?' is readily comprehensible; this does not mean that the answering is necessarily a very simple matter. But the question, 'Are you in favour of Britain entering the Common Market?' is also readily understood, even if all the implications of the question may be totally incomprehensible to the respondent. A gut reaction against entering the Common Market is a gut reaction against entering the Common Market. In a society which claims to be democratic, it is important to know the reactions of the public to policy issues, however subjective, emotional, and irrational they may be. The weight to be attached to such opinions is another matter.

Some more refined methods of measurement

The simple trichotomy of 'yes', 'no' and 'don't know' has worried most students of public opinion for some time, basically for the reasons outlined in the previous sections. Its intrinsic simplicity naturally has much to commend it to pollsters working on a limited budget, but that very simplicity, as they are themselves aware, does less than justice to the complexity of opinions. A number of devices have therefore been suggested for representing opinions in what might be thought of as a more realistic way. Once again, it is advisable to turn to the text-books for a full discussion of the various methods now employed by social scientists in their attempts to describe public opinion statistically. All I shall do is draw attention to some of the techniques employed by the pollsters themselves.

First, it may be useful to eliminate those expressions which are not opinions at all. Some polls use a filter to leave out those who are totally ignorant of the survey's subject-matter. The Gallup Poll, for instance, asked prospective respondents whether they had ever heard about comprehensive schools before asking those who had what their opinions were. Whether this really improves the quality of the findings is open to doubt. Only about ten per cent failed to pass through the filter, which is the same figure as Abrams calculated measured those who never participated in politics at all. It seems reasonable to suppose that about that proportion of the electorate would fail to answer *any* question positively. The difficulty is that the sort of filter which we are now considering implicitly posits that the respondent ought to have heard of the topic and thus encourages him to say that he has. It can do little or nothing to obviate the problem of those who feel obliged to express themselves but are thereby forced to choose their replies at random. The filter may be further developed by asking open-ended questions, thus preventing the respondent from being guided in his reply by alternatives suggested by the pollsters themselves.

Most techniques, however, are concerned with the second problem, that of differentiating between positive levels of intensity (the filter is aimed at excluding those who, having no opinions, have no intensity). One method is to provide the respondent with a simple continuum of possible response positions from which to estimate his own. This can be done by verbal or non-verbal scales. A verbal scale would allow the respondent a choice of, say, four positions: very satisfied, moderately satisfied, moderately dissatisfied, and very dissatisfied. There is some controversy over whether a middle resting place should be provided; to force a person to take sides may be to pressurize him into a category to which he does not genuinely belong; to provide a compromise position may be to absolve him from making a decision at all. What should be avoided is a bias on one side or the other of the middle point. An example of this failing was Gallup's choice of the following three possible positions: very important, important, not very important; important is not a neutral resting-place, but a positive expression of approval. The vital symmetry between favourable epithets and unfavourable ones must always be retained. As a rule, only a small proportion of questions are asked in this way, although in Germany some of the polling has been extensive, detailed and discriminating (Neumann and Noelle, 1962). The Gallup Poll once introduced a sophisticated methodology, called the quinta-mensional plan. This involved five stages, a filter to test awareness of the topic, open-ended questions, questions with a limited choice of answers, an interview in depth aiming to discover reasons for holding certain opinions, and finally a continuum on which to measure intensity (Gallup, 1948, 40–9). It proved too complicated and expensive to be commercially workable.

With most systems aimed to establish intensities, every opinion is initially given the value of one; it is not therefore actually concerned with *measurement*, which implies scales to differentiate between individual items, but with the process of *counting*. The answers to each possibility in our single continuum are counted and expressed as a percentage of all the responses. This will certainly give us a fuller picture of the public's opinions than the more common yes-no dichotomy, but the figures are still, like the polls, simple aggregates which tell nothing about the relative weights of each category. This fundamental distinction between counting and measurement can be illustrated by an analogy. One forest may have more trees than another, but the other may be composed of larger, more mature trees and thus consist of more timber. To decide which was the bigger forest would require a decision on whether we were carrying out a census of trees (counting) or were estimating existing timber supplies (measurement). Opinions may be thought of as trees, with one vital difference. There is no recognized scale, like cubic footage, with which to measure them.

Scientific measurement is supposed to be objective, but most scales are self-rating, and therefore subjective. The verbal scale is one example; so are most non-verbal scales. In these cases the respondent is presented with a graphic scale of, perhaps, eleven squares, one end indicating extremely favourable and the other extremely unfavourable. He has to indicate where on this scale his opinion lies. The pollsters sometimes use this method when attempting to discover the public's views on leaders' individual qualities. It is comparatively simple, but it is imprecise. Precision requires, apart from a greater degree of objectivity, a scale of measurement allowing different values for different answers. The leader rating index undertaken by Marplan attempts to do this; each respondent is asked to indicate where on a five-point scale he rates a particular leader for the quality of, say, integrity. Each point is given a set value and the values are aggregated for all respondents on all the questions and an average score is then calculated. That is the leader's rating. This implies that the gap between the categories 'very satisfied' and 'moderately satisfied' is equal on our continuum to that between 'moderately satisfied' and 'moderately dissatisfied', an assumption which is more convenient than demonstrable. Nevertheless, even if the mathematical precision of such devices is called in question—and measuring, David Butler has reminded us, is for the measurable—these various methods do help politicians to make some sort of estimation of the intensity with which opposition to their policies is held.

By raising the sort of questions which we have in this chapter, we have implicitly suggested that the public opinion which the pollsters measure, or count, is not perhaps a very useful definition. With its emphasis on one man, one opinion, one value, it seems to ignore the disturbing facts that some people hold no opinion at all, and others hold their opinion more strongly than many of their fellow electors. If polls aim to describe statistically what the public is thinking, they must take this into account, even if it is inconvenient. And yet, running through most debates on the polls is a confusion between what public opinion *is*, ill-defined, élitist, immeasurable, and what public opinion ought to be, articulated, democratic, and above all sufficiently measurable to be published. It is to this that we must now turn.

5

Public opinion polls and British representative democracy

So far we have discussed the polls which attempt to describe what opinions the public is holding only in very general terms. In this chapter, the focus moves on to the relationship between these polls and British representative democracy. At first sight, opinion polls appear to have an obvious function to perform in a democracy. We accept the right of every citizen to participate equally on election day in the choice of his nation's leaders; from this it is only a short step to accepting that every citizen should play an equal part in choosing his nation's policies, and opinion polls can give the governors a very accurate idea of what the citizens would like the government to do. This short step, however, involves certain difficulties. For many governmental decisions seem to be the concern not of the whole nation but of part of it; it has also been argued that in some areas of policy-making matters are so complex or secret that it would be wiser to entrust decisions to the experts rather than to the nation as a whole. In fact, the practice of British representative democracy has raised the status of the government to that of Burke's independently minded member of parliament. Our democratic theory, therefore, has to be reformulated to take account of this.

A democratic presumption stated

A presumption exists in most expressions of democratic theory that the governors should represent the views of the governed as far as is possible. 'The function of the government,' one pollster has written, 'is to provide for its peoples the way of life which the peoples themselves require' (W. Gregory, 1969). In the United Kingdom, so one theory of representative democracy runs, the requirements of the people are enunciated in electoral programmes and public approval is tested and expressed at general elections, when the electorate chooses those who will represent their wishes. The representative nature of the British member of parliament developed from the Burkean idea of an independently minded member whose wisdom his constituents trusted in all matters to what was in effect a delegate elected to transmit constituents' views to the seat of government. But, with the rise of mass parties, the citizens then elected a member whose prime responsibility was to support a set of leaders in carrying out a published set of policies. This theory of the mandate is no longer realistic (even if it ever was), but it remains a common part of the vocabulary of politicians, political commentators, and dissatisfied electors (Birch, 1964, 116–22).

Under the present system of representative democracy in Britain, direct influence which the governed may have had in the days of the delegate is now observable only at irregular intervals, sometimes five years elapsing between the isolated acts of nation-wide political participation provided for by general elections. The implications of this can be worrying, for a period of five years gives a government ample time to carry out policies of which the electorate does not approve and yet also time to sugar the bitter pill to receive once again the approval of the public at the next general election. What evidence there is suggests that, except in special cases it is only the performance of the government during its last twelve months that is influential in deciding which party the voters will support. Much of what a government does, therefore, receives neither approval nor, in the last analysis, repudiation. In January 1968, a correspondent to *The Times* expressed his disquiet at this in the following words: 'The British people have three more years of this government to go. . . . During this period they will be as effectively disenfranchised as they were under the Stuart kings.' Even if it is held that an electorate which endorses a government noted for its unpopular actions gets the government it deserves, it would remain true to say that the government had been acting in a way which was not representative of the public's wishes. One way of discovering the public's wishes in the intermediate period between acts of general participation is to use polling. This has the added advantage that the various policies lumped together in a single party's programme can be polled individually. In this way, it is argued, the findings of polls ought to guide, perhaps direct, those who make decisions in Whitehall or Westminster.

It is not always realized that the Government already has at its disposal the Government Social Survey to undertake research into public opinion. But it spends less than a million pounds a year on it and many departments actually go to the private polling organizations for their survey work. The director of the Government Social Survey has been quoted as saying that the Survey is inhibited because whatever it does 'must be politically defensible: that is to say, ministers must be willing to answer questions about it. The subjects investigated and methods of work must be done so that they can at any time be publicly discussed and defended' (W. Gregory, 1969). And there is not much evidence, as the next chapter suggests, that governments are willing to listen to the public's wishes if they differ markedly from governmental policy.

The use of the opinion poll, like that of the referendum, does seem to be highly democratic in that it increases enormously the communications between governors and governed. In an ideal situation, it might be thought, the leaders would follow the requests of their constituents, whose views, in George Gallup's opinion, are always eminently sane. After all, they accept the people's verdict at a general election; they should, therefore, accept the people's verdict between general elections. Public opinion, in other words, ought to be what the pollsters say it is, and not the public manifestations of influential persons' opinions, which academic scholars tend to study in their search for what actually influences decisions. The democratic presumption that all the people ought to be consulted all the time must, however, be looked at somewhat closer.

All the people all the time?

It is beyond doubt that all the people are not consulted all the time. While this may be defended on the grounds of efficiency and convenience, the fact must still be considered in the light of the democratic presumption, a widely accepted moral axiom, that governors should be continually responsive to the views of the governed. This presumption, carried to its logical conclusion, involves government by public opinion poll or referendum. Such a conclusion raises a number of theoretical difficulties which derive from the multifarious nature of political decisions in general.

Two such difficulties are illustrated by particular issues on which the British Government had to make a decision in the winter of 1967-8. The proposed siting of the third London Airport at Stansted provides the first illustration. The number of people directly affected by the

Government's original decision was but a tiny part of the whole British population, so that it could be argued that only these people, and not a random sample including citizens from Portsmouth or Manchester, was the appropriate public to consult. In other words, on some issues the appropriate public to survey may not be the nation but the *affected public*. But it is not as simple as that. This kind of decision can affect many more people in indirect ways and with varying degree of intensity, for the need to take a decision implies that the choice lies between building a third airport at Stansted, building it somewhere else, or not building it at all. First, the decision to build a third airport at all involves public expenditure, provided in part by the citizens of Portsmouth and Manchester. Should they not therefore be consulted about the uses to which their taxes are put, since the distribution of the national wealth is clearly a subject of intimate concern for all the nation's inhabitants? Second, problems arise if the affected public opposes the Government's decision. If this happens, a further, and probably unknown, proportion of the country's population is implicitly involved and their views are presumably worthy of some consideration. So long as the emphasis is laid on locating the airport at Stansted, their opinions might be given less weight than those living in the neighbourhood of Stansted, even if such a geographical locality could be reasonably defined. But their turn might come. Since it is highly probable that every site chosen would find more opponents than supporters in its immediate neighbourhood, a continuous procession of snap opinion polls in the areas successively nominated as possible locations would ensue. This would be expensive, decide only that there would be no decision, and so effectively annul the Ministry experts' appraisal of the national interest.

This introduces the second illustration, the planned development of the British Museum. During the controversy which raged over this, there were many who held that the opinions of the experts, whether in librarianship, research, or other academic fields, should outweigh the personal interests of the locality's inhabitants, even though the experts happened to be in a numerical minority. In other words, on some issues the appropriate public to survey may not be the nation but the *expert public*. The paramountcy of experts has been defended in certain fields, most notably perhaps in foreign affairs, where the general populace has normally been woefully ignorant (Rogers et al., 1968). Once again, difficulties arise. There is no simple and generally accepted rule which establishes the issues within the exclusive purview of experts. Indeed, the Government originally accepted the paramountcy of expert opinion over Stansted but accepted the paramountcy of affected opinion over the British Museum. Then, it is not always clear who the experts are; for example, should the appropriate regional planning authority have counted as experts in the Stansted case?

At first sight, therefore, there are some persuasive reasons for denying equal consideration to parts of the nation which are not directly affected by individual policies or which are not fully informed of the complications inherent in another policy issue. Furthermore, it is impossible to set definite criteria for selecting the public which might be polled. There are also other reasons why it may be inappropriate for public opinion polls to play any decisive role in an ideal decision-making process. For example, we may develop the implications from the last chapter by suggesting that some people's expressed opinions, because they are reflex actions, should not be taken into consideration. The quality and intensity of opinions varies enormously. The variation in quality is illustrated by the famous New Yorker cartoon in which a respondent is depicted replying to an eager pollster in these words: 'I'm afraid I have no opinion at the moment. All my journals of opinion have been late this week.' If the journals had been on time, should his opinions have been valued more highly? The variation in the intensity with which opinions are held requires no illustration.

Central to all these cases is the logistic problem of devising some scale of values to differentiate between the claims of variously affected publics or between the weight attributable to the experts in comparison to the laymen. Any mathematical method of ascertaining public opinion which does not impart to each individual, whatever the direct relevance of the problem to him, an opinion of more or less equal value is going to be very hard to invent and defend against objections.

This brings us back again to the pollsters' definition of public opinion, derived from one man, one vote, one value and transcribed into one man, one opinion, one value. Since every citizen has an equal right to take part in choosing the political leaders of his country, he should also have a right, the pollsters argue, to take part in creating a climate of opinion which the Government ought largely to follow. If a man's vote, cast without intellectual motivation, is valued as one in exactly the same way as every other elector's, surely his opinions, even if they are formed with an equal lack of intellectual motivation, should also be of the same value as those formed only after deep thought and much research. Similarly, since the least intense voter casts a ballot with the same value as the most ardent partisan, it is arguable whether great intensity of feeling should necessarily be given great weight in the opinion polls. Thus, the pollsters' definition is seen to be not merely convenient but also morally correct, since it reflects the practices of those sysmbols of democracy, the polling booth and the referendum.

While there can be little doubt that the definition is convenient, doubts can be cast on the extent to which it does reflect electoral practice. We find nothing undemocratic in not discovering for which party non-voters might have had a preference; surely, therefore, there is nothing undemocratic in suggesting that, if a man does not wish to take part in pressure group activities, such opinions as he may have, unexpressed and uncommunicated, need carry no weight (Plowman, 1962). It is the pollsters who force him to offer an opinion; he goes to the polling booth of his own free will. Perhaps this encourages the argument that a pollster's first duty is to ask the respondent whether he has thought about the matter at all, whether, in fact, he actually holds an opinion. On the other hand, it is less easy to participate effectively in pressure group politics than to express support for a political party at a general election. Opinion polls do allow many of the less privileged citizens to express opinions who would otherwise, through lack of access to pressure groups, be unable to do so.

Because of the nature of political issues, government by public opinion polls has at least two more significant limitations. In the first place, some method must be devised to discover the issues on which the public wishes its opinions to be consulted. At the moment the issues are provided by members of the expert public for the general public to comment upon. In the second place, and more importantly, most policy alternatives cannot be summarized accurately in a form suitable for polling. Surveys are best suited to provide insights into the general attitudes of the electorate; governments, on the other hand, require answers to specific problems with complicated and far-reaching ramifications. Popular participation is wholly appropriate in the choice of political leaders. The problem facing the electorate is then to decide which set of leaders it would prefer to carry out the intricacies of government; the choice, as all recent surveys on electoral behaviour have shown, is normally made in terms of general images, generally favourable dispositions towards one party, or general feelings that one party is the defender of 'my' interests. But when individual policy issues arise, it can be argued that general feelings are less useful than knowledge for making wise decisions. Of course, if the electorate was well informed, the situation would be different.

By suggesting that there may be a qualitative difference between choosing a set of leaders and deciding upon the merits or demerits of entering the Common Market, it becomes necessary once again to distinguish between the pollsters' concept of public opinion, general and negative in influence, and the academics' dynamic concept, élitist and positive.

Positive and negative public opinion

The most obvious occasion on which the pollsters' theory and the practice of British politics cohere is during a general election campaign. For here the object of the prediction itself assumes that every elector's vote is valued the same. However, apart from these predictive polls, the public opinion which operates positively in British society takes into account that individual opinions can be variably valued and that many sections of the community may, because they lack strong commitment, be conveniently ignored. The determination to go ahead with the attempt to enter the EEC, for example, was encouraged not by the number of the general public who actively supported this policy but by the lack of a widespread opposition, and the considerable size of the uncommitted. Deciding that the polls indicated that the general public was apathetic and knowing that the policy would not stir up concerted and vociferous opposition from opinion leaders, the Government felt able to forge ahead with few fears of internal dissension. As Lord Windlesham summed it up, 'evidence had emerged suggesting that not only was an articulate élite representing a strong body of informed opinion favourable, but that popular opinion too was unlikely to prove incorrigibly hostile' (Windlesham, 1966, 157). Positive, or informed public opinion as it is sometimes called, is élitist; governments as a rule *do* pay more attention to the experts, to the vociferous and to the active.

This is not to say that general public opinion, the pollsters' variety, is devoid of influence. Gone are the days, it is true, when men like Lord David Cecil could genuinely believe that 'the most powerful weapon at the command of the League of Nations is not the economic weapon or the military weapon or any other weapon of material force, but Public Opinion'. General opinion by its very nature cannot *make* a government react by its own positive stimulus any more than Chief Justice Marshall's pronouncements could *make* Andrew Jackson abide by the Supreme Court's judgments. Nevertheless, politicians in a country with a political culture like Britain's do take notice of shifts in general public opinion, essentially because they need the public's support in order to retain power, or regain it, at a general election. Thus the general public enjoys the negative power of withdrawing support from those who had previously been chosen as the country's governors.

We must, therefore, distinguish sharply between two types of public opinion, the positive, informed kind and the negative, general kind, not only by drawing attention to their different status but by pointing out the different nature of their contribution to British democracy. The parallel with elections is immediately striking. For here, most of the positive activity in creating policies, influencing leaders and encouraging the faithful is done by a group of experts or vociferous activists with strong views. The mass of the electorate merely records their acceptance, or otherwise, of one set of positive performers. The functioning of public opinion is analogous. Informed and positive activists create the issues and form the initial climate of opinion, but, in the last analysis, the pollsters' variety of public opinion may negate the activities of these leaders by being so overwhelmingly opposed to a project that the Government, or Opposition for that matter, with an eye on a future general election feels obliged to give way. The public opinion polls, in fact, have in part taken over from the civil servants their 'duty' to tell the Minister what the public will not stand. 'The value of public opinion,' it has been said, 'lies not in its powers of initiation but of control' (Ginsberg, 1964, 128). Naturally, such a generalization needs to be treated with caution. Immigration control, for example, may be seen as a rare example of the general public directly influencing a governmental decision; but even in this case the initiative lay not with the many, but with the few. And there are many examples where apparently hostile public opinion has been quite unable to control the government. The basic truth remains, however, that essentially national policies depend not upon the general public's hopes but upon the arguments of the informed public.

This distinction may be developed further. General public opinion is a function of informed opinion. It is essentially derivative, since it depends for its articulation upon a reaction to problems and policies presented to it. This bears a close resemblance again to general elections where the electorate judges what it is given to judge. Naturally, informed opinion is conscious of, and itself reacts to, general opinion in the same way that governments are conscious of, and react to, the electorate's mood. But the driving force, the positive creation of ideas upon which the many can form opinions or ultimately pass judgment in the polling booth, comes from the few, from the policy makers and the opinion leaders. The general public's influence is thus negative for the most part, for it merely approves or disapproves what is presented to it by the pollsters or the party leaders at election time.

Since this is so, it becomes doubly important to enquire into the source of the topics on which the public is asked to give its opinion or judgment. To give added weight to the results of polls might entail that the British system of government would degenerate into government by the pollsters, since they would decide both the subject and the form of the question to be asked. A method of impartial control could, of course, be devised; but, more important, some means of popular initiative to circumvent the difficulties arising from the derivative nature of general public opinion is required. And this would be completely contrary to the traditions of British representative democracy, for, with its suggestion that the wisdom of the few may override the wishes of the many, the British political system acknowledges the very different roles which informed and general opinion play in the practice of politics. Perhaps we should reconsider, therefore, the initial democratic presumption with which this chapter started.

A democratic presumption reviewed

Although democracy is intimately linked with numerical concepts like majorities and pluralities, in Britain the taking of political decisions is never thought of as a mathematical exercise. It is not difficult to discover reasons for this. In the first place, there is a general feeling that opinions are not the sort of things that can be quantified without so simplifying them that a distorted picture of a very complex situation emerges. It was the difficulty of devising a scale to measure the difference between individuals' expertise or the degree to which they might be affected by an issue which forced us to accept that the only possible scale of measurement was a strictly egalitarian one. And it was exactly because this scale seemed inappropriate that a more sophisticated one was sought.

In the second place, political activity in Britain has traditionally aimed to produce a balance between competing groups within society. The resulting consensus may represent the positive wishes of a relative majority or it may have been limited by the positive disapproval of certain groups within the country. In either case, public opinion polls, by ascribing positive views of equal weight to many who are in fact uncommitted, distort the true balance of opinion and may not therefore offer that acceptable consensus which conflicting pressure groups attempt to ensure.

In the third place, it is generally accepted that governments do have the duty to trust their own judgments and lead the public. It is only if this is accepted that governments can justify actions which reflect neither current public opinion as represented by the polls nor the policies presented at the previous election. The system of elected government operating in Britain is in effect government by competing élites (Schumpeter, 1950). The choice offered to the voter in the polling booth may be a significant one to many electors and all politicians, but it does not decide what policies a government follows. It merely determines who chooses them. In these four-yearly moments of public participation, the counting of heads after the style of opinion polls is deemed appropriate. After the election, however, the government arrogates to itself the Burkean right to owe the electorate its judgment rather than its obedience.

This represents the eternal dilemma of any democracy. Frequent conflicts between the wishes of the whole nation on specific issues on the one hand and the demands of efficiency, the national interest and what is possible on the other cannot be avoided. If a majority of British citizens are found to oppose the Concorde project, believing the government has got its priorities wrong and fearing the prospect of sonic booms, can a government continue such a project on the grounds that the alleged benefit is future technological growth to the whole nation's ultimate advantage? If a majority of the electorate supports the reintroduction of capital punishment, can a government continue to oppose a demand which it alleges is wrong, morally and practically? The conflict fails to materialize only when the national interest, efficiency and what is possible all coincide with the wishes of a majority of the nation's citizens; and this does not often occur. In Britain, the dilemma has been resolved by the acceptance of the maxim that some things are too arcane, too complicated to be left to the people; in these cases, the Government leads and the people follow. But the ultimate sanction remains partially with the people, for it is they who endorse the leaders they are forced to follow.

It would be naïve, however, to suppose that the Common Man has *no* say in deciding the issues on which the public is asked to express an opinion. Nevertheless, the basic truth remains that the translation of policies into legislation depends upon which set of leaders, offering views which the public has had little part in formulating, is endorsed. This endorsement gives the new government its legitimacy as well as a comparatively free hand. The public is thus seen to choose not representatives to further the interests of a particular localized group but representatives to support one set of prospective leaders. In such a situation, Burke's individuality approaches heresy. In other words, British representative democracy does not accept that the governors should be continually responsive to the governed; on the contrary, it implicitly acknowledges that the counting of heads is not always the most appropriate, or indeed wisest, way of making certain decisions; but on one issue the counting of heads is deemed to be correct. This is the choice of who are to be the leaders to make decisions on the more complicated issues facing the nation. British representative democracy is therefore seen to accept the whole country as a giant Burkean constituency. If we believe that this is acceptable in practice, that governments do have the duty to govern and lead the people, we cannot at the same time be surprised if the public opinion expressed in the polls is frequently ignored.

6

Polls and the politicians

We turn now from the general to the particular. The effect which public opinion polls have had on the functioning of the British political system has not been much discussed, but it seems to me that there are some areas of political activity where their advent has clearly had a marked affect. First, polls have introduced a new element into the effectiveness or otherwise of pressure groups. Second, polls have provided the Prime Minister with another formidable weapon, since they can help him to choose the most favourable time to go to the country. Third, polls have influenced the parties' electoral strategy, assisted their policy formulations, and been partially responsible for the movement towards 'consensus politics'. Finally, polls seem, as a consequence of this, to have enhanced the importance of the party leader.

The Government and pressure groups

Public opinion polls have probably affected British politics most significantly in the field of pressure group activity. Here they have an important role to play in defending the ill-organized many against the organized few; for the publication of opinion surveys ensures that pressure groups can no longer claim to enjoy the public's support if the polls indicate otherwise (McKenzie, 1958). In practice, however, this strengthens not the people's position but the Government's, since it is they who define on each occasion what is meant by public opinion.

Sometimes it is convenient to assume that the pollsters' definition is valid. The ease with which the Government overcame the anti-breathalyser lobby is a case in point. At one stage, Mrs Castle's new attempt to keep down the appalling and continuous increase in casualties from road accidents was presented as a flagrant infringement of the individual's liberty, which the public would not accept. This opposition, however, soon melted away, not only because the number of deaths on the roads in the two-hour period after closing time was reduced, but because the pollsters found that an increasing majority of the supposedly antagonistic public seemed to approve of an innovation like the breathalyser. In December 1965, fifty-nine per cent had been in favour of its introduction, a finding which almost certainly encouraged Mrs Castle to go ahead with her scheme; in January 1967, seventy-one per cent felt that the Government was not taking strict enough measures to deal with the problem of drink and driving and only a meagre five per cent maintained that the measures were too strict. Surely, the democratic argument ran, the public's approval overrode the interests of the brewers' lobby.

But sometimes the Government find it convenient to assume that the pollsters' definition of public opinion is not valid. The movement to restore capital punishment has been supported by a very large majority of the electorate. In July 1966, for example, seventy-six per cent of Gallup's sample favoured its reintroduction in cases of murder, eighteen per cent opposed the idea, and only six per cent failed to express any definite opinion. And yet there was no evidence, and hardly more likelihood, that Government policy would change. Informed opinion became the touchstone of government action; the experts, in morality no less than in criminology, were on the Government's side. They could argue that the vast majority of the electorate was insufficiently aware of all the relevant information, statistical and psychological, needed to form a wise and humane opinion on so complex an issue. It was not enough to base one's view on the belief that there had been on average more cases of murder each year since Parliament abolished the death penalty. Such a belief was itself based upon dubious statistics; but the essential argument that the death penalty was a deterrent was itself a debatable point. It was indeed still being questioned by those generally accepted to be the experts in such matters. In these circumstances, it was the duty of the government to lead opinion and not to follow it.

The debate in the House of Commons which decided that the Murder (Abolition of the Death Penalty) Act 1965 should not expire illustrates this argument admirably (House of Commons Parliamentary Debates, 16 December 1969, Cols. 1148–1294). Duncan

Sandys' claim that Parliament should not ride roughshod over the explicit and consistant views of the general public and James Callaghan's defence that there are times when Parliament has to act in advance of public opinion and give a lead are both well expressed in part of Sir Edward Boyle's speech. This is what he said:

'I agree that public opinion is highly important. . . . I should have thought that the figures of public opinion, so far as we know them, showed pretty clearly that public opinion does not want capital punishment to be finally removed from the Statute Book. . . . In my opinion, public opinion is fully justified in forcing the subject of crimes of violence on our attention in this House and demanding to know what we intend to do about it. . . . But there is one thing public opinion cannot do; it cannot force us in this House to vote for some particular measure that we are determined to have no part in. I see no inconsistency in saying that we should be responsive to concern felt by public opinion over a particular social problem, and that at the same time we are determined not to vote for something we feel with all our being to be wrong.'

To the active Parliamentarian, and more especially to the Cabinet Minister, the sovereignty of Parliament is sacrosanct. In this way, leadership in the face of public hostility can be justified and the people's elected representatives can, in the short run at least, positively misrepresent those who sent them to Westminster.

Nevertheless, the general presumptions about representative democracy require these to be excuses for not accepting 'the People's verdict'. These fall into four categories and are employed by all those, whether governments or pressure groups like the Trade Unions, who seek to influence the authoritative decisions of the legislature.

First, there can be a sceptical approach to the validity of the surveys themselves, even when various polls have produced similar results. 'You get the answers you expect,' George Woodcock is quoted as saying when asked his reaction to the consistently high support for introducing legally binding contracts into the field of industrial relations. Politicians like to think that it is they who have the direct line to the people. Not all of them, perhaps, would agree with Richard Crossman's famous comment that 'I am only completely convinced of the findings of the Gallup Poll when they confirm my own impression of what the public is thinking', but most, I suspect, would be prepared to use their findings as statistical backing for policies which they themselves support, but overtly at least, to ignore the unfavourable findings. Thus, in May 1969, a television addict could have watched a Labour back-bencher maintaining blandly that the polls just did not tell the truth and a Prime Minister implying that the unpopularity indicated by the polls did not really exist. These reactions are indicative of one effect the polls have had; as Bevan anticipated they would, they have deflated the politician's *amour propre* by removing from him part of his traditional role of the people's representative.

Second, there can be a firm belief that general opinion is so manipulated by the hostile mass media that the opinions expressed are not *genuine* opinions at all, but the product of the pressures exerted by society and the media on the individual. Let us take an example. As soon as the pollsters and newspaper editors perceived that the problem of unofficial strikes had become an issue at Westminster, they began to question the electorate at large for its views. Trade Union reform thus became Marplan's issue of the moment in its quarterly political survey carried out in January 1969 and special surveys were commissioned at the same time not merely of the general public but of particular publics as well, of trade unionists and trade union sponsored M.P.s. The results pointed in one direction only, that a majority of the electorate favoured legislation of some kind to curb unofficial strikes by accepting the main recommendations of Mrs Castle's White Paper *In Place of Strife*. These findings could be explained away in two ways. On one level, the electorate had been so conditioned by the news media into accepting the conventional wisdom of the times that they expressed opinions in favour of legislation, although before the issue became publicized, they had held no opinions. It is indicative that the majorities in favour of legislation diminished as its opponents began to be widely reported. On another level, it could be held that the particular issue, that of curbing unofficial strikes, was a bogus issue in that the correct order of priorities would not have placed it in the forefront of government policy objectives. It was the mass media which assumed there was a major problem; this it was argued, was open to dispute.

Third, and arising from this, some people may argue, as the Government argue over the reintroduction of capital punishment, that only a few people comprehend all the implications of certain legislative proposals. Thus trade union leaders could maintain that only they, with their intimate knowledge of industrial relations and their position as guardians of their members' interests, could speak with authority on the matter. Behind these positions lurks the fear that the masses do not, perhaps cannot, always make wise decisions. This view finds very clear expression in the Munir report of 1953 when the commission, commenting on the lack of education, experience and vision of the Pakistani people, concluded: 'In a country like ours, we have little doubt that the true function of leaders is to lead the people and not throughout to be driven by them at the head of the herd all the time.' Only in this way can the Government's policies on British Standard Time (but surely this was an issue readily comprehensible to the mass of the electorate) and decimalization be justified.

The final excuse, more often implicit than explicit, is that Governments must calculate the political realities and must necessarily compromise with powerful interest groups. To continue with the example of industrial relations, it might be said that the big battalions were represented not by the mass electorate but by trade union leaders and, to a lesser extent, by dissident members of the Labour party. In these circumstances, the broad mass of the people, if they do not have powerful allies, tend to take second place. What counts are political, not democratic, considerations. V. O. Key may be right after all to describe public opinion as 'those opinions . . . which Governments find it prudent to heed'. But the kind of clash which occurred over the Labour Government's Industrial Relations Bill is the exception, not the norm.

By and large, therefore, in contrast to the M.P.s' position, the Government's, based on its twin functions in the British political system of being responsive to popular demands and of shaping those demands, is in most circumstances enhanced. If the polls' findings are favourable, they can be used to vindicate policy and rout those bodies expressing views which the pollsters have shown to be opposed to the public's wishes. Once tarnished with an undemocratic label, a pressure group's influence is greatly reduced. If the polls' findings are unfavourable, the Burkean function of responsible leadership is invoked. A poll, after all, is not a referendum, which implies a high degree of obligation on the part of the Government to abide by the majority decision. Experience in Switzerland and Sweden, where the popular preference for continuing to drive on the left-hand side of the road was ignored by the Government, does not suggest that even in these cases Governments take kindly to popular opinion with which they disagree. There seems little doubt that opinion polls, which have no such obligation as the referendum implies, are likely to be ignored if the results do not reflect the views of the Government party's leaders. In addition, to bow to the statistics of public opinion polls is to by-pass the whole Parliamentary system; and that, Parliamentarians say, would be unthinkable.

The timing of general elections

The second development of interest is the way in which predictive polls have in theory enhanced the power of a Prime Minister. He can now watch the polls until they show a marked trend in favour of his party and then ask the Monarch to dissolve Parliament with every expectation of gaining a handsome victory at the subsequent general election. Furthermore, the tactics employed by both Government and Opposition may be dictated by opinion poll trends. The 1964–66 Parliament provides some evidence for this view, although obviously the Labour Party's tiny majority hardly makes this period a typical case. The Conservatives attacked in the summer of 1965 when they were shown to be holding a steady lead, in the hope that they would bring down the Labour Government and fight a general election with their star in the ascendancy. But when the polls began to swing against them, attacks from the Opposition became somewhat muted as they no longer wished to defeat the Government and fight an election which they would have expected to lose. Mr Wilson, on the other hand, having weathered the storm of that summer, was able to wait for the Conservative disarray in 1966 and the very favourable trend in the opinion polls (reinforced by the by-election success at Kingston-upon-Hull North). Understandably confident that he would win a greatly enlarged majority in the House of Commons, he announced the dissolution of Parliament on 28 February and won a considerable electoral victory a month later. In other words, the publication of opinion polls is an added asset which the Prime Minister can use to ensure that his party remains in office. If he watches the polls carefully, he may choose a time, perhaps a short moment in a four-year Parliament, to dissolve and receive once again the support of the British electorate. It is probably more important to emphasize the obverse of this, namely that opinion polls warn a Prime Minister when *not* to call an election.

The usefulness of this weapon depends very largely on two separate factors. First, the Prime Minister already has the right to ask for a dissolution by and large whenever he wishes. The British case is therefore different in kind from the United States of America, for example, where the date of elections is fixed and, for all intents and purposes, West Germany where there are, except in very exceptional circumstances, the same arrangements. At least, the assumption on which politicians base their electoral calculations is that the date for the next legislative elections is certain.

Second, the Prime Minister is already armed with the weapons of

Keynesian economics. Thus, as a Government's five-year period of office moves into its last quarter, it can effectively manipulate the economy to provide a small boom, satisfy the less ideologically committed electorate, watch for its popularity to be reflected in the polls and then go to the country. Both 1955 and 1959 fit this pattern satisfactorily. This can theoretically be done as well in countries where the legislature is elected for a fixed period of time; but in Britain, a Prime Minister has much more room for manœuvre. It is important, of course, that the economy should be able to stand a consumer boom in the months before an election. Between elections unpopularity may be so deep, however, that no amount of electoral management can remedy the situation and this danger is especially in evidence if the unpopularity begins in the second half of the Government's term of office. As Sir Alec Douglas-Home found in 1964, time does run out; but it was a mighty close thing.

Polls are almost certainly more accurate antennae of the electorate's pulse than the politicians' own impressions. One may query the exact precision of their figures, but the trends can usually be taken at face value. There may sometimes be conflicting evidence between the polls, as there was in 1963, when the major polls were moving in different directions. But this is rare. Normally, the indication which they provide of the electorate's temper can be accepted with confidence; a shrewd government of course would allow a few percentage points margin for statistical errors and second level voters returning to the party from which they had deserted. Prime Ministers before the Second World War might well envy their successors, for timing in those days remained something of a gamble. Nevertheless, it should not be thought that the polls, manipulated by the Government in some magical way, have a positive force of their own. It may be that a vote-catching budget will be followed by greater Government popularity and the upswing in the polls assist the Prime Minister in choosing the most suitable date for a general election. But if the electorate obstinately refuses to endorse a political party, there is nothing which that party's leader can do to stay in power indefinitely, however hard he watches the trends in the polls and stimulates the national economy. Time will run out for him too and repudiation at a general election will remove him from office, polls or no polls.

The parties and polls: electoral considerations

It has been said that politicians are always looking ahead to the next election. While this may be an overstatement, it is a strange man indeed who is not concerned about his party's image in the country and the likelihood of himself being re-elected in his constituency. Ministers, it is true, may concentrate on the ministries to the exclusion of the immediate problems of a general election, but their survival depends upon maintaining popular support with the public. In the last analysis, therefore, 'the vigilance of the Public', as a defeated minister once expressed it, 'operates powerfully on the sub-conscious of the Government' (Durant, 1955, 155). Efficient polling can tell a politician, and his party, not only how popular he is with the voting public but also where he is least popular and on what issues he loses popularity. Louis Harris has estimated that in the United States the intelligent use of surveys could make a difference of three or four per cent to a candidate's vote and thus, in his logically curious phraseology, actually 'alter the outcome of the election' (Harris, 1963, 6). In the United States many candidates for the Senate or the Governor's lodge no less than the White House have used private pollsters for some years. Although personal campaigns are not part of the British electoral tradition, the same techniques could be used for parties, but they came late to the scene and are still not widely employed, even by the Government itself before embarking on new policies.

The Conservatives were the first to break away from the traditional methods of electioneering. They had always been more ready than the Labour Party to employ the techniques of the advertising world; after all, as Lord Woolton himself once observed, the voter is also the consumer. The Labour Party, on the other hand, feared the new methods of collecting information as a threat to its ideological integrity and the member's mystical bond with the common man; the more managerial structure and sympathies of the Conservative Party enabled it to act upon the findings and advice of the communications experts in the 1959 general election (Abrams, 1963). Before this election, the party indulged in a large campaign of electoral propaganda couched in a language and illustrated with pictures suitable not for an activist élite but for the more apathetic majority. At this stage, intuition and impressions remained the chief source of information about the electorate; private surveys were only used as inquests after particularly disappointing by-elections or by the party's advertising consultants to copy-test an advertisement designed to sell the Conservative product as previously defined by the political leaders themselves (Rose, 1967). The Conservatives' victory in 1959 *may* be accounted for by their ability to convey their brand image successfully, but it did not depend on tailoring policies or issues to popular demand.

A hesitant step in this direction was in fact taken by the Labour Party. Actually, Gaitskell had commissioned two surveys from Mark Abrams's Research Services Ltd in 1956, but the opposition of Bevan and others on the NEC prevented any further surveys being undertaken, especially at a time when party unity was at a premium. The Conservatives' victory, the death of Bevan, and the steady strengthening of Gaitskellites in leadership positions converted many of those in authority to the view that opinion research and public relations were legitimate activities of political parties of the Left. In 1962, Abrams was allocated £5,000 by the NEC to undertake a survey on their behalf. *Socialist Commentary*, a pro-Gaitskell journal, had already sponsored one sample survey from Abrams which had confirmed the findings of academics that the majority of the electorate was neither intellectually nor ideologically motivated (Abrams and Rose, 1960). The Labour Party's campaign before the 1964 election could be distinguished from previous campaigns by the more professional approach of men like Abrams, although voices from the past were still to be heard inveighing against such developments (Samuel, 1960). The principle was accepted that most voters were more interested in *Z-cars* than political debate and that most people perceived politics in terms of improved housing, education, or pensions. Most important of all at this time, advertisements and slogans were rigorously copy-tested to ensure that they invoked favourable responses (Rose, 1967). The position of the party leaders was not, however, usurped. The surveys discovered what to concentrate on, which aspects of agreed policy should be emphasized; they did not attempt to re-create the product being sold.

This was one of the problems facing the Conservatives, for by 1963 it was not clear what constituted their product nor whose face should go on the package. Whereas it was normal to do survey work before unleashing propaganda, the Conservatives employed NOP to conduct some research into the characteristics of floating voters *after* the advertising campaign had got under way. It also seemed that the party had forgotten the lessons of 1959, for they returned to much more traditional, élitist methods of electioneering. Polling was used, but the leaders frequently trusted their own intuition more than the statistics of their research staffs (Butler and King, 1965). One reason for this was that the findings indicated that what interested the electorate divided the party (and Labour incidentally was thought to handle such issues better) and what the Conservatives were considered to excel in, foreign affairs, did not interest the electorate. Another, and far more important, reason was that once in office there seemed little time for party leaders, even if they had been interested in market research practices, to become involved in detailed research projects.

This general point is illustrated by what happened after Labour took office in 1964. The Labour Party indulged in virtually no survey work between 1964 and 1969 on their own account. In 1969, however, conscious of their continuous low rating in the opinion polls, they did hire an American expert in motivational research, Conrad Jameson, to help them discover the causes and extent of their unpopularity. In February 1970, the Labour party's general election campaign committee commissioned Research Services Ltd to undertake a survey of eighty constituencies throughout the country in order to isolate the issues on which the electorate felt most deeply. In contrast, the Conservatives in 1964 immediately undertook enquiries not only into the causes of their defeat but into the reasons why certain sections of the electorate continued to or ceased to identify with the party. This latter attempt to build a model of the electorate had not really borne any fruit by 1966; it was intended for use in planning the party's campaign for an election in 1970 or 1971. It occupied some of the time when the Shadow Cabinet met at the Selsdon Park Hotel in February 1970 to plan their strategy for the next general election. At the same time as this large, long-term research was developing, the party encouraged Humphrey Taylor, who had done some survey work for the Conservatives when working at NOP, to set up his own market research organization and then undertake smaller scale surveys. These activities of the Conservative Party serve to illustrate the great changes that took place between 1959 and 1969 in the methods of collecting information about prospective voters. Even the Liberals have commissioned surveys although never on the grand scale of the two major parties. They sponsored constituency studies for Colne Valley in 1963 and Ladywood in 1969.

Private polls are one method of collecting information, but the published polls can be used as well. Two instances where they played an important role in directing Conservative leaders' actions come to mind: the replacement of Sir Alec Douglas-Home in the summer of 1965, and the soft-pedalling of the comprehensive schools issue by the Conservatives in the 1966 general election, and 1967 Greater London Council elections. In July 1965, NOP found that the British public regarded Sir Alec as less sincere than Harold Wilson. This blow to what most senior Conservatives imagined to be Sir Alec's greatest asset was followed a week later by his resignation from the party leadership. It would be wrong to imagine there was a direct causal relationship between publication and resignation, but there seems little doubt that the poll hastened the day when Sir Alec was to give way to a new, and younger, leader of the party. Comprehensive schools were the subject of much polling; both the published and the party's private polls confirmed that twice as many people favoured comprehensives as disliked them. Although Central Office appears to have had some difficulty in persuading the party faithful not to emphasize their defence of the grammar schools, the national leadership played the issue down both in 1966 and 1967. They felt it was a vote loser, since their survey information indicated that it was to the uncommitted 'target' voters that the comprehensives appealed most. What polls have done is to help party leaders to escape from the restrictions imposed upon them by the partisan nature of their traditional channels of communication.

These new developments may have two far-reaching effects. In the first place, they could enhance the status and importance of the communications men whose position depends not at all on popular choice. As Butler and King put it, 'in order to discover what was palatable or what might be made palatable, the party had to discover what the tastes of the electorate were' and the means by which this was to be done depended upon the media experts (Butler and King, 1966, 65). They have not, however, misused their position as yet. The party leaders decide what the right policy is and the research is carried out in order to see how it can best be presented. They are concerned with where to lay the emphasis, not with suggesting policies to emphasize. In the second place, politics have become even more expensive. It is not that advertising and polling costs a great deal of money (a sample survey of 2,000 electors in actual fact is much cheaper than keeping one full-time agent in the field and probably quite as productive); it is that campaigns have become longer and more expensively mounted. For all the researchers, together with the accumulated experience of the professional advertisers, have shown that it takes time to impress upon the public particular brand images. Campaigns, therefore, are planned to last for at least a year, continually propounding the solid virtues of the party and leading to a crescendo a few months before the election. Election campaigns are not now limited to the period between the dissolution and polling day; they last much longer than that and cost more than even a decade ago. The polls assist in organizing them, draw attention to promising lines of propaganda and mould the overt image which the parties try to project. Fundamental policies, and therefore the underlying image, remain the prerogative of the politicians, who are still prone to exaggerate the importance of evidence about the electorate that they acquire from their own face-to-face contacts. Whether the next generation of leaders will feel so sure of their links with the people and the rightness of their principles is another question.

Towards a consensus

Abrams's two major research projects between 1959 and 1964 had different aims, but assisted in one development. The first project reaffirmed what academic research had already suggested and many politicians had begun to suspect: the electorate, by and large, was not concerned with ideological issues, whose language was not widely understood, but with more mundane matters within its direct experience. The second project was designed specifically to tell the Labour party more about the electors who held the balance of power between the monolithic cohorts which supported the two major parties so regularly. These 'target' voters were the uncommitted electors in uncommitted constituencies. They lacked demographic homogeneity and differed hardly at all in terms of age, sex, or social composition from the electorate as a whole. But, since they effectively held the balance of power between the great national parties, party propaganda and policies were aimed at attracting them. Paying attention to a particular category of voter was not actually a new development. Lord Poole had had a group of target voters in mind throughout the long campaign before the 1959 election (Windlesham, 1961, 249). The exact definition of the group in focus tended to change; Lord Poole's were youngish, newly married manual workers earning above-average wages and subjectively tending to think of themselves as middle-class; Abrams's were more socially varied and shared the common quality of living in marginal constituencies; the post-1964 Conservative survey sought out those who lacked party identification.

But they all had one thing in common, a non-partisan approach to politics. The major parties therefore sought to emphasize specific policies on the matters which did concern this middle group, housing, stable prices, education, and so on. The tactics of Conservative propaganda in 1959 were symptomatic of this new approach. The result has been that the public stand of the two parties has grown nearer together, so that in May 1963 the political editor of the *Sunday Times* was able to construct a composite advertisement drawn equally from Conservative and Labour advertisements, such that either party could have used a copy of it with no change other than the concluding slogan. To an outsider without a historical feel for British politics and with an unrelieved concentration on avowed policies, the two major parties might seem almost undistinguishable. He would, of course, be seeing only *part* of the truth; but it *is* part of the truth. By competing for the support of the target voters, the Conservative and Labour parties have narrowed the area of political debate.

The leaders and the polls

The tendency towards the middle ground, for which the polls may share some responsibility, has led to an increase in the attention given to the party leaders' standing in the polls. If many voters perceive politics as the process of deciding upon the less ideological problems of housing, health and general prosperity, and if they see that the rival parties are offering, within these limited spheres of personal interest, much the same products, they naturally find it hard, on these grounds at any rate, to decide which of two similar pro-grammes to support. Since unwavering commitment to a party is losing its compelling influence over a large proportion of the electorate, greater emphasis has been given to the image of the leader to differen-tiate between two parties whose advertised wares seem so remarkably similar. Butler and Stokes concluded their study of the electoral impact of the leaders between 1963 and 1966 by suggesting that strongly held views about leaders did affect party choice to a certain degree but that attitudes towards the parties emerged as the stronger influence (Butler and Stokes, 1969, 383-8). The responsibility for enhancing the status of party leaders is only partially the polls'. The mass media, and especially television, have encouraged it. Nor should we forget that the speed of modern communications has elevated the position of the Prime Minister still further over his colleagues by denying him excuses for not visiting foreign dignitaries. The spotlight on the Prime Minister forces the opposition party to build up their champion as well. Similarity of policy, the natural preference for personal loyalty, the enhanced status of the leader, all these make the public's approval of a party's leader of great import-ance.

The Labour propaganda before 1964 emphasized the personality of Harold Wilson, so that his face became familiar throughout the country. The unpopularity to which Harold Macmillan had suc-cumbed, itself a result of the communications revolution, prevented the Conservatives from advertising their champion (Rose, 1967; Abrams, 1964). The electorate may be ignorant about issues but it enjoys a slight knowledge and a considerable interest in personalities; the party and leader must therefore be linked. It is this necessity which makes a party leader seem almost impregnable vis-à-vis his backbenchers. Investment in the leader is so great that only the most reckless would challenge him.

The importance attached to the leader is epitomized by a new conventional wisdom which emerged in the middle 1960s. For a party to be successful at elections, the argument ran, its leader should be far more popular than his opposite number and more popular even than his own party. It appeared as though the political parties were themselves aware of this. Thus, Sir Alec Douglas-Home's resignation as leader of the Conservative Party was prompted by his apparent unpopularity as indicated by the polls; Mr Wilson's leadership was strengthened by the long lead he held over any potential rival. The elections since 1955 do seem to have followed this conventional pattern, but it would be unwise to draw any iron rule from this limited evidence. There remains the suspicion that in the 1945 election, for example, the Labour Party may have led the opinion polls relating to voting intentions without leading the polls concerned with the popularity of rival leaders. More recently, the Conservative Party's success in by-elections and local elections since 1966 occurred in spite of Mr Heath's low rating in the polls. But the political context was different from that existing at a general election. If the decline in Labour support during the period 1967-9 is interpreted as a natural anti-government movement and not a genuine change of allegiance towards the Conservatives, Mr Heath's rating takes on a new importance. He might have taken comfort from the fact that Mr Wilson's rating was almost as low; certainly at no time since polling was regularly undertaken have the leaders of the two major parties been so unpopular with the electorate. Although some by-elections did show a gross gain in votes by the Conservatives, on the whole the swing in their favour was due to widespread Labour abstentions, the typical act of a disillusioned second-level voter. There were few indications that the change of allegiance was likely to be stable over time. Indeed the Gallup Poll figures showed that an increase in the Conservatives' lead over Labour was mirrored by an increase in the number of 'don't knows' and avowed Liberal supporters. As Labour cut back the lead through the autumn of 1969, the Liberal and 'don't know' categories diminished.

This emphasis on leadership rating in the polls (all the polling organizations include a question about the respective party leaders) seems to me to be overdone. In the first place, politicians do not like to be driven at the head of the herd all the time. The polls may have been a catalyst for Sir Alec's departure, but more influential were the personal pressures of leading party members. They may well have been impressed by his poor showing vis-à-vis Mr Wilson, but that had not disturbed Mr Macmillan in the past. Although Nelson Rockefeller was shown by the polls early in 1968 to have a much better chance than Richard Nixon of beating a Democratic rival, the professional politicians preferred to choose their own man. In the second place, voter ignorance is such that any leader enjoys an aura stemming from his own position, but this aura of leadership passes like a royal crown to the successor, as Edward Heath's astonishingly rapid rise in popularity immediately after he succeeded Sir Alec Douglas-Home indicates. It is therefore no wonder that the pollsters have difficulties in pointing to any politician with a standing equivalent to that of his leader. It is noticeable that the most popular second runner to the party leader in the party popularity polls has consistently been the cabinet minister or member of the shadow cabinet most in the news. For instance, the second most popular Labour Leader among Labour voters in April 1968, following cuts in government expenditure and a severe budget, was Mr Jenkins; in April 1969, following extreme party disunity over trades union reform, he had been replaced by Mrs Castle. In neither case would an objective Olympian have selected these two as the most likely candidates for the second position. It was probably the exceptional public exposure given to Mr Powell in 1969 which raised him, briefly, into a position of greater popularity among Conservative voters than the leader of his party. The rule, however, seems to be that any potential rival is a long way behind his leader in the party popularity polls. In the third place, personalities have always played a major part in forging links between the electorate and the party, so that this is nothing new in kind. One has only to think of Gladstone and Disraeli, Chamberlain and Asquith, or Lloyd George and Baldwin to be reminded of the way in which British politics have traditionally been intimately linked with popular attitudes towards leading party members. The present-day emphasis is probably new in degree, but that is as much due to the communications media as to the polls. Nevertheless, the impressions created by the leader is probably one important influence affecting voting behaviour. The tendency towards Presidential politics, with opposition leaders making world tours after the American model, cannot however be laid wholly at the door of the pollsters, even if they have assisted in creating the apparent similarities between the parties from which the Presidential style has emerged.

The survey concluded

No survey of public opinion polls in Britain would be complete without a passing mention of their usefulness to students of politics. The monthly bulletins issued by Gallup and NOP provide a wealth of material about the public's expressed opinions. These have been used from time to time in this monograph to illustrate general points being made about political behaviour. We should remember, of course, that polls are descriptions, not explanations, and that the evidence from them can be used only to test hypotheses, or to draw attention to phenomena which require explanation. Statistics do not provide positive proof of the truth of a hypothesis, but they can give support to it or, if the findings contradict it, help to establish its untrustworthiness. The major impact of the polls, however, has unquestionably been in the actual practice of politics.

They have not, in fact, produced the benefits which their doughtiest supporters would have hoped. They saw that governments seemed able to act along lines seemingly quite unresponsive to the public's expressed opinions and quite contrary to the very promises on which, as most democratic theories presume, they were originally elected; and they seemed able to do this in Great Britain for a considerable period of time. In these circumstances, it was hoped that public opinion polls would ensure a continuous dialogue between governors and governed to be carried on between elections and that the roseate picture of citizens gathering in the agora to decide upon possible courses of executive action could be partially resurrected. This hope has remained unfulfilled.

Nevertheless, the advent of the polls *has* altered the relationship between the governors and the governed. Electors became aware both that they were thought to be of sufficient importance that people would spend money to discover their opinions and also that politics was important to them now that its content was essentially non-ideological. It is noticeable how both Gallup and Marplan have been asking the public their views on their standard of living on the broad theory that the electorate's sense of an improving standard of life is the best omen for the government. This emphasis on non-ideological matters is almost bound to result in a greater fluctuation in voting behaviour since the solid bases of unshakeable party support are in some measure eroded. When politics cease to be based upon deep philosophical commitment and the parties tend to be judged in the light of their attitude or performance on issues directly relevant to the ordinary elector, the chances of a return to the pendulum days of the late nineteenth century, when successive governments could hardly fail to alienate some of their supporters, might seem high (Mackintosh, 1962, 198–204). But it is not likely: Keynesian economics and the polls themselves provide the government with too many weapons for them to be caught out in the same way as their predecessors were a century ago.

The least important aspect of the polls, it seems to me, is the way in which predictive polls keep up a running commentary on the popularity ratings of the political parties. For one thing, it diverts attention from matters of much greater national importance. For another, little is gained by stressing that politics is a sort of horse race, when the odds are in a state of gentle, if perpetual, flux, especially since the last poll is published as the horses are within a couple of lengths of the finishing post. Nothing is gained by knowing approximately today what will be known accurately tomorrow. Much more useful is the light the polls can throw on the public's view on specific policy issues, the way in which people react to particular events and the kind of things to which the public say they attach the greatest importance. Even if we view the findings of the polls with some suspicion, as I am sure we sometimes should, they are certainly more accurate and objective representations of the hopes and aspirations, if not the emotions, of the nation than anything an individual reporter or politician, however sympathetic, can produce. The polls, in short, have taken over from the electorate's representatives the role of telling the political leaders what the voters are thinking.

This is to raise what may be termed the generic attack on polls. The overt precision of polling has certainly introduced a new dimension to British politics. There is nothing romantic or heroic, as Sir

Kenneth Clark once pointed out, in polls or computers. Indeed, to those who hanker after the romantic image of politics, in which great visions are presented to the people by men concerned above all with moral and philosophical issues, the polls are almost sordid. They destroy the mystical link between the representative and his constituents; they challenge the sacred supremacy of Parliament; they encourage an emphasis on shrewd electoral considerations at the expense of principles; they drive the parties into practising consensus politics. Such is the romantic's indictment.

Mystical links, however, offer no confidence to the unbeliever that contact has been made with a cross-section of society. There is little proof that politicians are impartial and accurate recorders of the sentiments even of those they meet; canvass returns, for example, are notoriously unreliable. We are not short of evidence to suggest that many politicians trust their own antennae and the impressions gleaned from chance acquaintances on week-end journeys to their constituencies rather than the cold statistics presented by the research experts at party headquarters. The most skilled commentator, despite a flair for conveying atmosphere, cannot discover the views of a statistically representative sample of the electorate in the way an opinion poll can. The systematic process of collecting responses which the best survey techniques employ does provide a far more reliable guide to actual conditions, opinions, or intentions than people's impressions. The polls may take the poetry out of politics, but they also inject a little more objective evidence into it.

The romantic, indeed, has always lived in a world tainted with not a little arrogance, for his claims to knowledge, whether of moral truth or of constituents' wishes, is based only upon his own intuition. It can also be argued that if the people's major concern is with the more immediate problems of housing or prices, it is the duty of the politicians to cater for this concern. This has fine democratic overtones; but it does ignore the old argument that a politician's duty is not merely to be the people's mouthpiece but also a leader intent on changing accepted opinions. Bringing politics down to essentially non-ideological issues rather than to arcane principles of political philosophy, it has been argued, 'is to mobilise the interest of millions of otherwise apathetic voters' (Abrams, 1964, 19). Turnout statistics do not support this thesis; on the contrary, the move to consensus politics, by blurring the distinction between the two major parties, may in effect have denied to much of the electorate a meaningful choice. In any case, consensus politics can have dangerous products. Just as the Grand Coalition in West Germany encouraged the spawning

of splinter groups on both extremes of the political spectrum, so
in Britain front bench collusion, by removing some issues from the
arena of public debate, may well have encouraged movements outside
the normal constitutional channels. So even the pragmatist may have
his doubts about the benefits of the opinion polls.

Finally, we should not ignore the potential of opinion surveys. The
tactics and success of John F. Kennedy's presidential campaign in
1960 were due in no small part to the skilful use and understanding of
these new techniques (White, 1961). It has been claimed that Winthrop
Rockefeller 'went out and put Arkansas in his carpet bag with the
aid of the first computerised political campaign in American History'
(Chester, Hodgson and Page, 1969, 215). And there is some evidence
that computerized data were largely reponsible for the image which
Nixon's advisers successfully projected of their candidate in the 1968
Presidential Election (McGinnis, 1969). Political parties in Britain
have been much less intrigued by their potentialities for discovering
voters' foibles and thus planning campaigns; partly for historical
reasons; partly because the uncommitted voters, while vitally
important, have been few in number; partly because the style of
politics is much less personalized. But there are dangers. It may be
that survey findings will establish that it is not the programme but
the personality of the candidate or the techniques for promoting
him which attract the target voters, so that electioneering becomes one
giant sales drive. Indeed, one of the major tactics of the Labour
Party in 1964 was to push Mr Wilson as the symbol of the party. It
may be possible to promote with success unscrupulous candidates
whose interests lie not in translating their programmes into legislation, but merely in acquiring votes to secure a position of power for
themselves. Of course, history has plenty of examples of power being
acquired according to the constitutional procedures by unscrupulous
men who made no use of opinion polls.

Nevertheless, power through opinion polls is not a fantastic vision.
Eugene Burdick has described with frightening realism the way
in which the skilful use of polling data, psychological research,
and promotional techniques could be harnessed, through a computer,
to sell a candidate. 'I believe a person ought to say what he thinks,'
the hero of his novel says at one stage, 'and not what a machine tells
him some large group of people fear or some other group of people
love' (Burdick, 1964, 272). Yet ambition finally triumphs and the
potential of the Simulmatics Corporation's computer remains. There
is something distasteful in the thought of British politics degenerat-
ing into a competition between two groups of electoral manipulators,

each eager to attract at any price the support of that section of the electorate without ideological conviction. As the standard of living in Britain gradually rises, we may expect this section to increase. The logical outcome, perhaps, is that we shall see in Britain a counterpart to Hal Every, whose Los Angeles advertisement ran as follows: 'You can be elected Senator; leading public relations firm with top flight experience in statewide campaigns wants a Senator.' The likelihood of such a novel practice coming to Britain seems slim; the historical weight of tradition which still dominates British politics, the comparative unimportance of personalities other than party leaders as vote catchers and the present attitudes of both active politicians and party research officers are opposed to this sort of development. But, as long as the major parties compete for the middle ground, the possibility remains. That is, in itself, an indication of the importance and the reliability of the opinion polls.

Appendix

Gallup Poll: May 1969 (Selected Questions) circle appropriate code

A. (i) If there were a General Election tomorrow,
which party would you support?

1. Conservative
2. Labour
3. Liberal
4. Nationalist
5. Other
6. Don't Know

(ii) If *Don't Know*: Which would you be most
inclined to vote for?

7. Conservative
8. Labour
9. Liberal
O. Nationalist
X. Other
Y. Don't Know

B. Were you able to go and vote in the General
Election in March, 1966 or were you prevented? *Ask all who voted:* For which candidate did you vote?

1. No, did not vote
2. Yes, voted for Conservative
3. Labour
4. Liberal
5. Other

C. Do you approve or disapprove of sending
British troops to Northern Ireland to guard
key installations?

1. Approve
2. Disapprove
3. Don't Know

D. If an opportunity occurs for Britain to join the   1. Try to join
   Common Market, would you like to see us try   2. Drop the idea
   or drop the idea altogether?   3. Don't Know

FURTHER READING

There are no books devoted exclusively to public opinion polls except George Gallup's own work, *A Guide to Public Opinion Polls* (Princeton, 1948). Many general books now include chapters on them, such as F. Stacey, *The Government of Modern Britain* (Oxford, 1967), R. L. Leonard, *Elections in Britain* (Van Nostrand, 1968), and, most useful of all, the various Nuffield Studies of British general elections.

On general problems connected with definition, development and manipulation of public opinion, the two classic texts, W. Lippman, *Public Opinion* (Penguin, 1946) and W. Albig, *Public Opinion* (McGraw-Hill, 1956), should be consulted. Three more recent volumes are B. Berelson and M. Janowitz, *Reader in Public Opinion and Communication* (Collier-MacMillan, 1966), H. L. Childs, *Public Opinion: Nature, Formation and Role* (Van Nostrand, 1965), and R. E. Lane and D. O. Sears, *Public Opinion* (Prentice-Hall, 1964). Books on the statistical techniques of polling and survey work are legion. In my view C. A. Moser, *Survey Methods in Social Investigation* (Heinemann 1958), remains the most useful, but F. Conway, *Sampling* (Humanities, 1967), F. Yates, *Sampling Methods in Censuses and Surveys* (Griffin, 1960), and W. G. Cochran, *Sampling Techniques* (Wiley, 1963) introduce the subject with various degrees of difficulty.

Most of the relevant literature, however, apart from the monthly bulletins prepared by Gallup and NOP, is to be found in journals, especially the *Public Opinion Quarterly*. Each section of this book contains references to the most useful articles on its topic, but it might be helpful at this stage to nominate eight out of the bibliography as being particularly worthy of note. In chronological order, they would be: Harrisson, 'What is Public Opinion?'; Speier, 'Historical Development of Public Opinion'; Durant, 'Public Opinion, Polls, and Foreign Policy'; Samuel, 'Dr. Abrams and the End of Politics'; Rose, 'Political Decision-making and the Polls'; Plowman, 'Public Opinion and the Polls'; Converse, 'New Dimensions of Meaning for Cross-cultural Sample Surveys in Politics'; and Bogart, 'No Opinion, Don't Know, and Maybe No Answer'.

Finally, one work of fiction will repay the reading: Eugene Burdick, *The 480* (Gollancz, 1964).

Bibliography

Abrams, M., 'Public Opinion Polls and the British General Election', *Public Opinion Quarterly*, xiv (1950), 40–52.

Abrams, M., 'Social Trends and Electoral Behaviour', *British Journal of Sociology*, xiii (1962), 228–42.

Abrams, M., 'Public Opinion Polls and Political Parties', *Public Opinion Quarterly*, xxvii (1963), 9–18.

Abrams, M., 'Opinion Polls and Party Propaganda', *Public Opinion Quarterly*, xxviii (1964), 13–19.

Abrams, M., and Rose, R., (1960), *Must Labour Lose?*, Penguin.

Albig, W., (1939: 2nd edition 1956), *Public Opinion*, New York: McGraw-Hill.

Allen, A. J., 'Voting recollections and intentions in Reading: an opinion poll experiment', *Parliamentary Affairs*, xx (1966–67), 170–7.

Beck, K. W., and Savaray, J., 'From Bright Ideas to Social Research: Studies of the Kennedy Assassination', *Public Opinion Quarterly*, xxxi (1967), 253–64.

Berelson, B. R., Lazarsfeld, P. F., and Mcphee, W. N., (1954), *Voting*, Chicago: University of Chicago Press.

Birch, A. H., (1964), *Representative and Responsible Government*, Allen and Unwin.

Bogart, L., 'No Opinion, Don't Know, and Maybe No Answer', *Public Opinion Quarterly*, xxxi (1967), 331–45.

Booth, C., (ed.) (1889–1902), *Labour and Life of the People of London*, 17 vols., Macmillan.

Bowley, A. L., 'Working-class Households in Reading', *Journal of the Royal Statistical Society*, lxxvi (1912–13), 672–701.

Bromhead, P. A., 'The General Election of 1966', *Parliamentary Affairs*, xix (1965–66), 332–45.

Burdick, E., (1964), *The 480*, Gollancz.

Butler, D. E., (1963), *The Electoral System in Britain since 1918*, Oxford.

Butler, D. E., and Rose, R., (1960), *The British General Election of 1959*, Macmillan.

Butler, D. E., and King, A. S., (1965), *The British General Election of 1964*, Macmillan.

Butler, D. E., and King, A. S., (1966), *The British General Election of 1966*, Macmillan.

Butler, D. E., and Stokes, D., (1969), *Political Change in Britain*, Macmillan.

Cantril, H., (1944), *Gauging Public Opinion*, Princeton: Princeton University Press.

Cantril, H., (1951), *Public Opinion 1935–1964*, Princeton: Princeton University Press.

Chester, L., Hodgson, G., and Page, B., (1969), *An American Melodrama*, The Literary Guild.

Childs, H. L., (1965), *Public Opinion: Its Nature, Formation and Role*, Princeton: Van Nostrand.

Cliffe, L., (1967), *One Party Democracy*, Nairobi: East African Publishing House.

Cochran, W. G., (2nd edition 1963), *Sampling Techniques*, New York: Wiley.

Converse, P. E., 'New Dimensions of Meaning for Cross-cultural Sample Surveys in Politics', *International Social Science Journal*, xvi (1964), 19–34.

Conway, F., (1967), *Sampling*, Humanities Press.

Durant, H., 'Public Opinion, Polls and Foreign Policy', *British Journal of Sociology*, vi (1955), 149–58.

Gallup, G., (1948), *A Guide to Public Opinion Polls*, Princeton: Princeton University Press.

Gallup, G., 'The Changing Climate for Public Opinion Research', *Public Opinion Quarterly*, xxi (1957), 23–7.

Ginsberg, M., (1964), *Psychology of Society*, Methuen.

Gregory, R. G., 'Local Elections and The Rule of Anticipated Reactions', *Political Studies*, xvii (1969), 31–47.

Gregory, W., 'Let the People Choose', *New Statesman*, 24 January, 1969.

Harris, L., 'Polls and Politics in the United States', *Public Opinion Quarterly*, xxvii (1963), 3–8.

Harrisson, T., 'What is Public Opinion?', *Political Quarterly*, xi (1940), 368–83.

Hyden, G., (1968), *Tanu Vajenga Nchi: Political Development in Rural Tanzania*, Uniskol, Lund.

Johnson, B., 'Ascetic Protestantism and Political Preference', *Public Opinion Quarterly*, xxvi (1962), 35–46.

Jowell, R., and Hoinville, G., 'Opinion Polls Tested', *New Society*, 7 August, 1969.

Key, V. O., (1961), *Public Opinion and American Democracy*, New York: Alfred Knopf.

Leonard, R. L., (1968), *Elections in Britain*, Van Nostrand.

Lowell, A. L., (1919), *Public Opinion and Popular Government*, Longmans.

Mackintosh, J. P., (1962), *The British Cabinet*, Stevens.

Macleod, I., 'The private world of political science', *The Times*, 30 November, 1969.

McGinnis, J., (1969), *The Selling of the President*, Trident.

McKenzie, R. T., 'Parties, Pressure Groups and the British Political Process', *Political Quarterly*, xxix (1958), 5–16.

McKenzie, R. T., and Silver, A., (1968), *Angels in Marble*, Heinemann.

Milne, R. S., and Mackenzie, H. C. H., (1954), *Marginal Seat*, Hansard Society.

Milne, R. S., and Mackenzie, H. C. H., (1958), *Straight Fight*, Hansard Society.

Moser, C. A., (1958), *Survey Methods in Social Investigation*, Heinemann.

Moser, C. A., and Stuart, A., 'An Experimental Study of Quota Sampling', *Journal of the Royal Statistical Society*, cxvi (1953), 349–405.

Mosteller, F., et al., (1949), *The Pre-election Polls of 1948*, New York: Social Science Research Council.

Neumann, E. P., and Noelle, E., (1962), *Statistics on Adenauer*, Allensbach: Verlag für Demoskopie.

Pickles, W., 'Psephology Reconsidered', *Political Quarterly*, xxxvi (1965), 460–70.

Plowman, D. E. G., 'The Public and the Polls', *The Listener*, 14 January, 1960.

Plowman, D. E. G., 'Public Opinion and the Polls', *British Journal of Sociology*, xiii (1962), 331–49.

Qualter, T. H., 'Seats and Votes: an Application of the Cube Law to the Canadian Electoral System', *Canadian Journal of Political Science*, i (1968), 310–35.

Rogers, W. C., Stuhler, B., and Koenig, D., 'A Comparison of Informed and General Public Opinion on US Foreign Policy', *Public Opinion Quarterly*, xxxi (1967–8), 242–52.

Rose, R., 'Political Decision-making and the Polls', *Parliamentary Affairs*, xv (1961–62), 188–202.

Rose, R., (1967), *Influencing Voters*, Faber.

Runciman, W. G., (1966), *Relative Deprivation and Social Justice*, Routledge & Kegan Paul.

Samuel, R., 'Dr. Abrams and the End of Politics', *New Left Review*, No. 5. (1960), 2–9

Schumpeter, (1950), *Capitalism, Socialism and Democracy*, Allen and Unwin.

Speier, W., 'Historical Development of Public Opinion', *American Journal of Sociology*, lv (1950), 378–88.

White, T. D., (1961), *The Making of the President 1960*, Cape.

Windlesham, Lord (Hennesy, D. J. G.), 'The communication of Conservative Policy, 1957–1959', *Political Quarterly*, xxxi (1961), 238–56.

Windlesham, Lord, (1966), *Communication and Political Power*, Cape.

Yates, F., (3rd edition 1960), *Sampling Methods in Censuses and Surveys*, Griffin.